DON'T PUSH ME,
I'M NO COMPUTER

Other Books by Helen L. Beck

Social Services to the Mentally Retarded
Going to Camp: A Guide to Good Camping

DON'T PUSH ME, I'M NO COMPUTER

How Pressures to "Achieve"
Harm Pre-School Children

by Helen L. Beck

McGraw-Hill Book Company
New York • St. Louis • San Francisco
Düsseldorf • London • Mexico
Sydney • Toronto

To my nephew, Andy Ungar

book design by Marcy J. Katz
Art Director: Robert L. Mitchell

1234567890   BPBP   798765

Library of Congress Cataloging in Publication Data

Beck, Helen Louise.
Don't push me, I'm no computer.

  1. Education, Preschool.   2. Academic achievement.
3. Motivation in education.   I. Title.
LB1140.2.B42   649'.1   73-7930
ISBN 0-07-004233-0

First McGraw-Hill Paperback Edition, 1975

ACKNOWLEDGMENTS

Acknowledgments seem always insufficient. One can never really acknowledge one's debt to the many people who have helped in shaping one's opinions, stimulating one's thoughts, and influencing the conclusions one draws. One may not always agree with those one listens to, but one respects them and is aware of their influence.

Out of the many, I do want to give special thanks to those among my friends and my co-workers who have debated with me, have drawn my attention to material in support of or in conflict with my approach, and have dropped a continuous stream of newspaper clippings and magazine articles on my desk.

I want to thank especially those who have taken time from busy schedules to read the manuscript and make valuable comments. I am particularly grateful to Anna Freud, who had much influence on my early professional development and has now graciously given time and effort not only to read the manuscript but to write the Foreword.

I want to thank Claire Gold, Assistant Superintendent for Pupil Personnel and Special Education of the Westport Board of Education. Her understanding and support of my approach has been very meaningful to me. Both she, Dr. Lillian Mould, Mrs. Emma Plank, and Miss Cornelia Goldsmith have offered generously of their time and thought to read and discuss the manuscript. I also want to thank Sandy Spangler and my nephew Andy Ungar, the two young people who provided a different point of view.

CONTENTS

FOREWORD

The welfare of children has become a matter of public interest in our time, and numerous institutions have been called into being in every corner of the world to safeguard the interests of children of all ages. Obviously, with this increase in programs, an ever-increasing number of adults is necessary to plan, organize, and staff what has been created and to amend and supplement parental care.

There is no doubt that parents and professional workers are in need of additional knowledge and that not all the available literature on child development is suitable for the purpose of staff training. Much instruction can be given to the involved adults by observation and practice on the job, but, ideally, this should be enlarged by the printed word dealing with the processes of maturation, growth, and development in general of children's basic needs and of the child's changing requirements for satisfaction of his wishes, control of his impulses, and structurization of his personality.

It is in these latter respects that this book makes a valuable contribution. The author, as an experienced teacher in the field and a school social worker, succeeds in a most satisfactory way to combine two major purposes. On the one hand, she presents the reader with an impressive quantity of detailed information regarding physical arrangements, toys, games, and occupations. On the other hand, she does not let the reader forget that these matters are no more than the technical props which assist the task of upbringing and that the real educational process does not depend on them but on the child's own rate of growth, on the gradual unfolding of his innate potential, and on his personal reaction to the stimulation offered to him. She emphasizes that no effort should be made to enforce development on any single part of the child's personality; that cognition does not prosper except in close alliance with emotional development, just as the drives and affects interact continually with the increasing functioning of the child's rational personality.

Above all, the author wages war with a tendency present in the modern world to replace contact with human beings by contact with mechanical devises. She argues that the latter may stimulate the child but that they do so impersonally and impartially, without regard to personal needs and characteristics and without opening up the opportunities for interchange which are a vital need of the human young. Provisions of this kind run counter to our knowledge that all the potentialities of human beings develop only on the basis of intimate interchange with living people. Infants and toddlers do not wake up to an interest in the surrounding world except by focusing first on a single person, the mother or caretaking adult. Only when security is gained and developed in this first relationship does the child reach out further and establish contacts. If he is denied the fulfillment of this basic need, he may remain uninterested, dull, and wholly involved in sucking, rocking, other rhythmic activities, i.e., in the pleasures which he can obtain from his own body.

The author reverts to this point repeatedly, pointing out the opportunities for development which are neglected under such conditions as well as the very real dangers to which many children of the present generation are subjected.

Anna Freud

INTRODUCTION

We think of young children as being very fast. Any young mother can vouch for the fact that her two- or three-year-old can get into trouble more quickly then she can catch up with him to prevent damage.

Actually, young children are not all that fast. It is just easier for them to run than to walk, to grab than to reach. They dash hither and yon and respond like lightning to their impulses. The reason is that running and grabbing require less muscle control than walking and reaching, and response to impulse requires no thought or control. When it comes to establishing controls, to understanding requests or demands, to thinking before acting, young children are slow. They are slow in absorbing a request and responding to it; slow in integrating experiences and transferring knowledge from one learned concept to another.

Adults, fascinated by the child's quick reactions to familiar situations and his often amazingly bright conclusions, are inclined to forget that these are flashes of awakening perception and not yet well-organized and integrated knowledge. To push knowledge and experiences on young children who still lack the neurological, physical and emotional maturity to absorb and organize can play havoc with their orderly development. We seem to have forgotten what we discovered only a few decades ago: namely, that the child is not simply a small adult but a very different being biologically, physically, and psychologically. To understand his outlook on his environment and his logic needs much sensitivity and love. Besides love, children need time and space for harmonious development.

This book is a plea to stop pushing children beyond their stage of maturation and allow them the time and environment within which they can unfold and develop into whole people to the best of their ability—and enjoy the process while they are growing.

Many of the illustrations and examples in the book are gleaned from the media that confront us all daily—the newspapers, television, radio, and advertising. We all read and hear the pronouncements that come over the radio or TV into our living rooms, and we easily absorb them as truths if they are repeated often enough. It is important to take a second and critical look at some of what we hear and see.

Helen L. Beck

1.
MECHANIZED CHILDREN

What you can't grasp does not exist for you;
What you can't count, that you think is not
   true;
What you can't mint you think will never
   pay;
And weightless to you is what you can't
   weigh.
(Was ihr nicht fasst, das fehlt euch ganz
   und gar;
Was ihr nicht rechnet, glaubt ihr, sei nicht
   wahr;
Was ihr nicht waegt, hat fuer euch kein
   Gewicht;
Was ihr nicht muenzt, das glaubt ihr, zaehle
   nicht.)

—Goethe

1

This is a rather free translation, with due apologies to Goethe. But, old as the verse is, it has special application today when we attach so little value to the subtle qualities in life that can be neither researched, nor quantified, nor tabulated.

THE NÜRNBERGER TRICHTER

Trichter means funnel, and legend has it that in olden times, probably during the Middle Ages, the good city of Nürnberg (Nüremberg) in Germany had in its possession a big funnel—the famous Nürnberger Trichter—with which to funnel instant knowledge into the dense heads of its citizens. The city was much envied throughout Europe for this device, though legend does not disclose whether the honorable citizenry of Nürnberg was particularly known for its wisdom. If it was, this wisdom has been lost to history, just as the funnel seems to have been lost. The only memory that remains is the German verb *eintrichtern* (literally, "to pour in through a funnel"). The connotation is "forcing knowledge."

The search for the Trichter has continued through the ages. There have been substitutes, but never again the real thing. It may be reassuring to us that other times besides our own searched for mechanical means to transmit "instant knowledge" and create the "instant sage" without much effort on part of teacher or pupil and that they too returned to more traditional methods of dispensing knowledge. It has been left to our own technical era to find a real substitute for the Trichter. The twentieth-

century model of the Trichter comes in various forms—
TV and radio sets, teaching machines, films, etc. There is
undoubtedly justification in the use of machines in providing information and as adjuncts to teaching. It should
give us pause, however, to see machines increasingly
substituted for human contact; to observe the attempt to
employ machinery to "program" young minds; to use it
to teach children shortcuts and hand them end products
before they have an inkling that there is a process in the
compilation of facts and before they can develop working
patterns of acquiring information.

In our fascination with the potentials of the new toy,
we are inclined to forget that machines dispense only
information and, therefore, have a tendency to dehumanize. Information is neither knowledge nor wisdom. It
lacks the enrichment, pleasure, and possibility of variety
of applications that are part of real knowledge, and it does
not add to the development of human values that are a
dimension of wisdom.

Today's Nürnberger Trichter has a menacing quality.
It is not the simple instrument of times past that belonged
to the authorities and had rather limited application. The
twentieth-century instrument has many forms and wide
distribution. It has become too convenient a substitute for
human endeavor and involvement. Mechanization and
automation deeply affect all our lives in almost all
aspects.

There was a time when we would have been frightened
to see unfeeling, unresponsive machines that are in the
long run uncontrollable take over for human endeavor.

3

Because of the propensities and the pervasiveness of these machines, and because of the current attempt to substitute them for real life experiences in children, we need to take careful stock of their reach, their impact, and their long-range consequences. We need to try to estimate not only the immediate and obvious effects that can perhaps be researched but the subtle, insidious ones that may defy tabulation. We must keep in mind that young children lack the support of previous experiences. They have nothing to fall back on when the machines fail them; in consequence they begin to suffer from the sterility of machine contacts. To counteract what automation may do to them, we must provide them with rich, tangible, human experiences, to make sure they develop the ability to find value in simple things. They will need constant opportunity for actual, three-dimensional encounters with people and with real feelings, positive and negative ones, in their real life setting. Artificially created groups are at best surrogates for life.

Machines today are thrusting themselves between the child and his tangible environment. They create for him a one-dimensional world of words, and a two-dimensional one of shadows and puppets. They present him with cartoon feelings that mean little to him, because he has not yet experienced them himself to any degree. They teach him that there is a simple, unfailing solution for any problem or hurt, even for those problems the child has experienced and found overwhelming. Machine problems are always somebody else's and solutions are always achieved in thirty minutes, giving the child an off-center slant on his expectations of life.

The thrust of the information explosion and the peculiarities of the machine age put great weight on the importance of accumulation of facts. This is creating tremendous adult anxiety. There seem to be too many facts to be learned and too much limitation of the human mind to encompass them all. It is quite possible that the adults are trying to master their own anxiety by force-feeding facts to the young.

Researchers are impressed with the young child's ability to learn. Newspaper reports indicate that research claims almost any child can be developed into a genius by well-focused efforts that make children reach their full potential quickly. This may be a simplification by news reporters on material they are reviewing, but, since it appears in print, it is quite persuasive to parents and possibly to the inexperienced educator as well. Such studies may confuse absorption of information with learning and see "potential" only as a quality of the intellect. They propagate full exploitation of the young child's abilities to store information. They bombard the child with facts that he does not yet understand, and for which he does not yet have any application. They also overlook the fact that the child's potential may not be in the intellectual area at all, but in areas to which little attention is being paid such as art, physical prowess, etc.

The use of machines seems the appropriate medium for the full exploitation of the child's ability to store information. Many of these machines are set up to prevent the child from making mistakes. Machines do not become impatient or bored. They may even hand out lollipops as rewards for achievement. The child thus can have endless repetitions and reruns, and he can pile fact upon fact in his mind—while his other abilities may atrophy.

Full exploitation of young minds is as dangerous as any kind of full exploitation. It drains the individual. It is bound to dull curiosity. It may channel abilities into a single, predetermined channel in accordance with and limited by the programer's imagination and abilities. And it may dry up springs of special gifts that are yet buried and unrecognized. It will create hybrids instead of well-rounded, live, multifaceted people. It might be argued that many children, if not trained by machines, are currently not developed by any other means. This does not make machine drill any more desirable.

Being fascinated by the machine's neutral and objective approach to children, we might remind ourselves that human shortcomings in the human teacher are not without their value. In contact with the teacher, the child experiences the give and take of real relationships. The human factor of fatigue in the teacher has its counterpart in the fatigue in the child. Thus, one can respond to the other, and the young pupil may be protected against being overloaded with stimuli by the adult's limitation in endurance. The sensitive teacher, whether he instructs the child in memorizing numbers, matching shoes to feet, or pedaling a bicycle, will know when the child has reached the limit of attention and endurance. He can stop. He, thus, may have given the child not only a lesson in a certain skill, but have provided, in a subtle, unobtrusive way, a lesson in perceptiveness, empathy, and human responsiveness.

The machine can do neither. It may endlessly repeat numbers and letters for the child to parrot. It does not know when to stop and how to dispense meaningful praise or correction. A lollipop that pops automatically out of a slit when the answer is right is a poor substitute for a parent's lively pleasure over the child's first effective use of the toilet, or over the first inkling the youngster gives of an awakening sense of another person's need or mood.

Maturation is a slow process. A fact that does not sit well with our impatient times—times which have such technical know-how of speeding up processes. Pressure cooker methods applied to live children may backfire badly. But the backfire may be considerably delayed and not easily connected with a single cause. Still, the damage may be far reaching. We already see a generation of youngsters unhappily struggling against fragmentation and alienation. These symptoms might be related, at least in part, to the intrusion of the machine and the lack of human involvement by those around them.

It seems that even young children do no longer automatically turn to adults in time of stress. A rather distressing example of this was reported by the press not so long ago. A first-grade teacher had discussed with her young pupils the feeling of anger and how they handled it. Most children's method of handling was isolating themselves rather than turning to the adults near them for help. Answers included such "solutions" as:

Go up to your bedroom and cry.
Lay on your bed and suck your thumb.
Hide under your bed.
Take a walk or run around in the yard.
Go away.
Go read a nice book, etc.

Only one child out of fifteen who suggested solutions said, "Tell my mother."

It is a distressing sign of our times when the young have been fed so many clichés that are supposed to help with overwhelming feelings that they have lost trust in the adult who can help them.

This is alienation that occurs in children who are exposed to TV as the mechanical baby-sitter in their early years, taught by teaching machines and wookbooks later on, and become anonymous numbers within too large a group at too early an age.

Young people may protest and overtly denounce guidance as interference. But they desperately want the effort, interest, and involvement of the adult. They do hear what is said to them, even as they defend their independence. When the right time comes they will select what will be serviceable to them and what they have absorbed from environmental guidance. Human involvement is not a candy machine that produces a neatly wrapped package on the insertion of a coin. Results are slow in coming. Cause and effect cannot be clearly and singularly spotlighted. It takes much varied and subtle involvement and time to produce a single reasonably able and satisfied human being.

Mechanized Children

There is a current trend in the management of children, and people in general, that takes a jaundiced view of emotions. The proponents of this philosophy state in essence that, since emotions can be neither tabulated nor quantified, they do not exist. The premise is that only the expressions of emotions can be researched and these expressions can be readily changed. What is obviously missed in the process is the fact that even what cannot be measured can exist; that overt expressions of an emotion may be misinterpreted by a researcher who denies the basic concept of emotions and knows little about the individual whom he is researching; that pat answers only look as if they fitted all situations; and that the overt expression of an emotion may change without any change in the underlying feeling.

Changes in feelings may indeed be achieved. Modified behavior may make a person easier to live with and, therefore, more likable. All of us respond to being liked (which, by the way, is also an emotion that cannot be measured). If accepted and liked, we feel less troubled about ourselves and, therefore, are less trouble to those around us. Changes also may be effected by the real interest and involvement of a therapist and researcher. It is not the M&M* he feeds the child everytime the youngster has responded, but the adult's liking of him

*Behavior modification is an approach to changing outward behavior in children and adults by immediately rewarding acceptable behavior. In children, this frequently takes the form of popping an M&M into a child's mouth as soon as he has given the right response, much as a fish is fed to a trained seal, or a nut to a trained bird who has performed.

and his wish to see him improve. M&M changes may not go beyond the stage of the tangible reward. Changes brought about by human involvement are likely to be more lasting.

Those of us who believe in the human quality of life find the existence of emotions confirmed by daily experiences with them, even if nobody has ever seen a feeling or knows where in the body it is located.

Heaven help us if we should ever be in a position to breed out of the human race all that is human. I hope we will never be able to replace either our marvelous spontaneous feelings—or even our shortcomings—with mechanical precision knowledge. Mechanically learned responses may shield us from the experience of deep sorrow and hurt. They may also do away with experiences of deeply felt joy and pleasure. They will dehumanize us as they deprive us of the satisfaction that comes from emotions shared with other human beings, and the deep enjoyment emanating from imagination that can also not be quantified. It is the tragedy of many so-called disturbed children or adults that they have never developed or have lost the capacity to feel deeply about themselves and others. To help them, we have to search for modes to reconnect them with the buried springs of deeply felt human relationships. These, also, cannot be achieved with mechanical means.

Mechanical means may bring fairly quick, even dramatic results. These are seldom lasting. Pressure cooker methods applied without the individual's involvement may be experienced as assault and may easily result in a change of defenses, rather than in a change of basic adjustment. The profile of this season's fashionable emotional problems differs considerably from those of a decade ago. This is only in part due to our cultural changes. We have seen too often that, as therapists develop means of coping with one set of problems, an entirely new crop develops to baffle them anew. (An example may be found in hysteria, which practically disappeared as a syndrome as soon as it could be fairly successfully treated.) As Christopher Robin would say: "How to amuse them today?"

I have seen young children in modification programs catch on to what the adults were about and take full advantage of the adult—not the therapy. Good therapy cannot be mechanical. The effective therapist has to be alert and responsive, so that he can be a step ahead of his patient and modify his own approach as needed. The same is true in all education. Routine responses turn the child off. Mechanical praise or reward may be equated by the child with lack of interest. Mechanical punishment may tempt him to manipulate the situation.

Our concern over the mechanization of child rearing is heightened by the fact that the young child, who is most exposed to such an approach, is particularly vulnerable. He has not yet experienced the real depth of emotions and his immature ego would not be able to handle their full onslaught. Love, concern for others, and meaningful relationships are developed only gradually as the child matures and finds himself the object of such feelings by those around him. The environment's spontaneous pleasure with his successes and its disapproval of unacceptable or callous behavior help him internalize such emotions so that they become part of his own personality. If he is not the object of love and interest, he cannot experience joy or anguish for those around him, nor develop the ability and desire to give pleasure to others or to avoid hurting them. He will thus remain superficial, empty, and in the long run dissatisfied. The young child has not yet developed the inner resources to which he can turn at times of discouragement. Internal resources, which are the springs of resilience and adjustment, are developed slowly. The time to assist in their development is in early childhood. If we pre-empt the child's early emotional *Lebensraum* too soon with sterile information that is as yet useless to him, he will not have time, leisure, and the uncluttered mind needed to develop character and personality.

I am thinking about a delightful one-and-a-half-year-old who, standing in the kitchen with his mother and her friend, was intently watching the mother. She was leaning against a cabinet, with her feet slightly crossed. There came an excited, "Look, look!" from the child. He had just succeeded in copying his mother's stance. This was a big achievement for him and was greeted with pleasure by the adults. Had the time with his mother been taken up "teaching" him coordination and body position, he would perhaps have learned all kinds of things earlier. It would not have had the joyful impact this piece of body control had on him. Nobody would have thought of teaching him just this specific skill. It was this achievement that gave him such joy because of his closeness to his mother, his wish to copy her, the achievement of a step in body control, and the mother's pleasure over the whole configuration.

In contrast to this delightful, spontaneous scene, I have watched a segment on *Sesame Street* where teaching is very purposeful and goal directed, and small, spontaneous achievements are devalued without any sensitivity toward a child's reaction to such an approach. In this particular segment, Big Bird is attempting to show off a piece of body control he has just achieved. The premise was similar to the one described before. The effect was rather forced and unfortunate. Big Bird is large and awkward. He was bragging about his achievement of being able, I think, to hop on one foot. His claim was, as it might well be with a young child, that he could do something that was very special. His pleasure was immediately dampened by the adult and the children to whom he demonstrated. Big Bird's pleasure over an achievement of a skill was quickly quashed in a rather crude way. It seems to me that the lesson taught to the young children who watched it was, "Don't expect anybody to share your pleasures. They will only make fun of you."

After this, since *Sesame Street* is a "morality" show, there were attempts to make Big Bird feel good again, and this too, was strained and artificial. Adults at times feel that the program is amusing. It seems to me that the amusement created by watching *Sesame Street* is the amusement of adults who find the shortcomings of an awkward child funny. They laugh about the child, not with him.

In the light of all this, we need to take careful stock of the current push to make all childhood experiences part of structured teaching and neglect the need to help the child develop spontaneous experiences that grow out of the interrelationship between people, life situations, and maturation. There is too much push for the acquisition of cognitive information onto ever younger children, and too much attempt to supplant people who are meaningful to children with mechanical teachers. There is too much bombardment of children with stimuli they are unable to absorb and against which they cannot defend themselves.

THE MECHANICAL TEACHER

The onslaught of modern machinery onto the field of child rearing, the intrusion of the franchised "Education Industries" and mechanized "Entertainment Factories" into the lives of young children ought to give us pause. There is much research going on as to the effect of the media on children and on their development. This raises a number of questions. What children are meant by this designation? Three-month-old infants, toddlers, teenagers, children with rich experiential backgrounds, neglected ones? Even with these questions clarified, a number of questions remain.

Research into human behavior and into the long-range effects of intervention in the development of children is a most difficult undertaking. Obtaining hard facts on subtle shadings has many stumbling blocks. The group to be researched and the control group cannot be fully matched. There are always subtle contaminating factors that cannot be either pinpointed or screened out. "Halo-factors"* and the requirements of the setting within which the research is conducted color the outcome of the findings. The very objectivity of the researcher may make him too detached toward his subjects. In human research such detachment may be difficult to achieve, and, if achieved, it may be at the expense of the human qualities of the researcher.

Research findings relating to the effect of mechanized teaching on children, TV in particular, is quite contradictory. The teaching value of TV is overrated by those who program to exploit its teaching potential, while it is minimized by others who feel criticized for ramming advertisements down children's throats or fill the screen with violence.

The children do learn, but much of what they "learn" is not what was intended by the programers. Programs like *Sesame Street* point with pride to the fact that they teach three- and four-year-olds letters and numbers by means of TV. The claim is that such early learning makes for brighter children. Such claims are supported by studies that imply that what Johnny does not learn during the first four years of his life he will never learn. What tragedy to have the prospects of life and its potential

---

*Halo-factor is a phenomenon well-known to psychologists; it occurs when they react subjectively to the research subject, e.g., to the considerable charm of a child or to extremely rude reactions of a test subject.

end at such an early age! If early learning is so important, that kind of teaching should provide the child with building blocks that are not dead ends, but lend themselves to further development of curiosity, interest, and personality. Cognitive information alone will hardly fill the bill. But it is cognitive information that the teaching media propagate.

Sesame Street graduates may indeed know their numbers and letters by the time they reach school age. But they have not learned what to do with this information. They often don't even suspect that there is a purpose or application for the material with which they are presented. Their excitement and curiosity about school may have been diminished. What information they have acquired has come to them, as it were, magically, without effort on their part. They now understandably expect this to continue. Learning as a participatory activity is foreign to them. They have missed the thrill of acquiring knowledge by mastering difficulties one step at a time. They sit back and wait for the magic. If it does not occur, they are sure that there just isn't anything more to learn—like the five-year-old who stated she was quitting school after a month because "she knew it all."

To many a child whose early learning and experiences centered around the TV with little parental involvement, school becomes an enlarged TV set. It is to provide entertainment and to be turned on and off at will. The teacher and the other children can be screened out of consciousness like the shadows on the TV screen. In many a home the set is on all day. Parents defend this by stating that the child pays only sporadic attention to it. He is thus trained for inattentiveness.

There are three- and four-year-olds who are in front of the set for up to six hours a day. What do they really do during those passive hours? Do they understand what they watch, or do they even try to understand? They may turn themselves off and daydream, suck their thumbs, rock. They may move away to other half-hearted activities against a background of noise and fleeting shadows. They may turn back to the screen from time to time snatching bits and pieces, never realizing that there is a sequence of events. Their experiences are fragmented and disorganized.

"What's a mother to do?" says the commercial. Reinforcing passivity in young children is a dangerous thing. At a time when they should be physically and mentally active and should develop sound patterns and foundations for living and learning, young children spend empty hours in the family car, in front of the TV, and, on Saturday, at the movies watching life go by. Instead of struggling to discover a world which for them is just the day after creation, they are handed predigested packaged information where their very questions are anticipated and they can memorize pat answers. There are no surprises and no errors that might lead to unexpected discoveries.

The physical effect of such encouraged sedentary living for the very young is alarming. Many doctors find related orthopedic and eye problems, as well as early signs of developing heart problems. The constant background noise and the persistent bombardment with stimuli that cannot be absorbed result in irritation, overstimulation, and pent-up energy. Frustration may consequently break through in unchanneled outbursts of aimless yelling, running, and a restless inability to settle down to any quiet activity that requires attention, concentration, and structure.

These children often demonstrate considerable hyper-activity, fragmented attention, lack of concentration, problems with *Gestalt,* inability to grasp certain three-dimensional concepts. Since these symptoms are familiar to us in the child with mild brain syndrome, it is quite possible that these children are lumped in with children with minimal brain dysfunction—though their problem is not a brain dysfunction at all, but a TV syndrome.

Surprisingly to those of us who are involved with young children, the effect of TV violence on youngsters is still subject to controversy. Large groups of parents, educators, and psychiatrists demand reduction of violence in TV programs directed at children. It is a limited re-quest asking for reduction, not exclusion. Commercial producers of shows give lip service to this need and some-times make token adjustments. Unfortunately, there is no clear, straight line between cause and effect that can be easily measured. The dynamics, however, are clear enough for those who are able to observe and wish to modify the causes.

Screen violence has its defenders, even among some professionals involved in the education and therapy of children. They argue that violence is part of our atavistic

18

past and, therefore, necessary to our well-being; that children have always enjoyed violence which provides them with the necessary catharsis from frustration; that violence previously was fed to the young with fairy tales and Mother Goose rhymes without harming them.

Without denying these facts, one would have to consider some errors of deduction in this kind of reasoning:

—One cannot escape the impression that we are already dealing with a group of experts, programers, and researchers who have been raised on movie, radio, and TV violence. They seem no longer really able to recognize violence as such or find its effects alarming.

—Without denying the cruelty and violence in fairy tales and Mother Goose rhymes, there is a decided difference between a story heard and a program seen. The young child of the pre-TV era was presented with the fairy tale by an adult narrator. The tale was absorbed only auditorily without visual reenforcement. The child listened without having to cope with the visual representation of gory detail. If the dragon's head was cut off, the child provided the imagery in accordance with his own maturity and experience. Since he had no experience with beheaded dragons, the imagery was likely to be within his coping ability. What may be presented to him on the home screen by adults with their own needs to present violent detail to young children is not.

—The story teller was usually an adult with whom the child was familiar. He may indeed have been identified by the child as the aggressor in the tale—the mother with the bad step-mother, the father with the cruel king—some other female with the witch. But at the same time the familiar adult could be trusted to switch roles and become the protector as the need arose. (Such ambivalence regarding an adult's role is quite natural to the young child.) The narrator who related to a particular child, or group of children could and would modify the story to tone down tension and anxiety in his particular audience. Once a child is old enough to read the stories himself, he is also old enough to distinguish between reality and fantasy and begin to cope with the material.

—Live story tellers were likely to tire after a tale or two and end the story hour. They would not grind out story after tale after program, piling horror upon horror as the machine is doing now. One might not be able to tabulate the cumulative effect of such TV fare, but it is clearly observable.

—In the fairy tale it is usually the witch, the dragon, or the wolf that gets killed. On the screen, violence is directed at everyday people, and not only the "baddies." There have to be several victims before badness is established. The gap between a child's daydreams and actual life is dangerously narrowed.

—Young children of halfway stable families had little familiarity with violence and killing before the TV era. Death, if they were unfortunate enough to experience it, was a real and very personal tragedy, not an ingredient of entertainment. Death has become pedestrian to today's two- to four-year-olds. I once overheard a rather startling conversation between two four-year-olds. They were peacefully painting at a double easel. Ellen said in a conversational tone, "I had a boyfriend, but he died." Richard peered around the easel and asked matter-of-factly, "Did the cops find his body?" It was a chilling experience to see those two cherubic, well-protected tots so casual about this topic. The little boy took it completely for granted that the boyfriend had come to a violent end. How can we expect children to be shocked at killings and violence if they absorb such events before breakfast in the morning, during the dinner hour at night, or anytime in between?

So much for the callousness developed by child-directed "entertainment." But children live with adults who have their own favorite programs. News comes into the living room with all the gory details the child might have missed at the "kiddie show." To the newscaster, it is all in a day's work. He may announce that there was a mine disaster or a shoot-out in the street, and that he will bring details of these and other stories. The child becomes inured against catastrophe, which after all is only a "story." He may also get accustomed to hear descriptions of a major plane disaster interrupted by a cheerful whistle and a song extolling the marvelous effect of a hair tonic or a digestive pill.

"What's a parent to do?" asks the commercial.

And so we hear that TV violence does not have a detrimental effect on children—at least not one that can be measured before and after. A newspaper story reported on an experiment with a group of monkeys. They were exposed to TV and found to go berserk after watching violence on the screen. But these apparently were monkeys, not children.

Monster shows are such favorites with children that parents cannot believe they could have a detrimental effect: "He wouldn't watch it if he were scared." Children's reactions to screen terror are often ambivalent. They may identify themselves both with the attacker and the victim and find some vicarious pleasure in the terror. They may almost compulsively repeat the experience without being able to stop on their own. If the adult steps in and rules out such a show, the child may go through the motions of protesting. The sensitive observer, however, will note the sense of relief that the thrill is over.

Parents of a six-year-old recently expressed great concern over the violent night terrors the child had suddenly developed. Because of some of the detail they described, I suggested that the daily monster show be eliminated. The parents were doubtful that there could be any connection. The child adored the show, they stated, and would resist any curtailing of his TV privileges. They were amazed to find that the youngster quietly accepted the restriction and that the night terrors disappeared almost immediately. The child never again asked to see this program.

Just as the child early develops callousness against suffering, he is also said to develop a crust against the onslaught of advertising. According to one study, children become cynical very early about the advertising that is thrown at them at regular intervals as long as they watch TV or listen to the radio. If this is true, is this cynicism desirable at such an early age? (The researcher indicates that even toddlers reach this stage.)

The young child's first contact with deliberate, bald-faced lying may indeed come to him via the home screen. TV personalities whom he admires and believes will literally try to "sell him a bill of goods." I remember the shocked remark of a three-year-old who, while watching a commercial on TV, turned to her mother exclaiming, "Mommy, this man is lying! He is lying!" What do we do to the moral standards of our children? And to their ethics? And to their value judgment in terms of human values and relationships?

"You have to have this doll to show off to your friends." "How will you make friends if you are still the only boy on the block without a banana seat on your bicycle?"

The implication is that the doll is not for play but for showing off. People like you for your possessions. Parental love is evidenced in terms of buying, buying, buying. The thrust against the child's weak sales resistance is unconscionable.

"What's a parent to do?"

The hotly desired toy that looked so glamorous on the

screen turns out to be shoddy, it is difficult to manipulate, and it breaks almost before it is unpacked. The talking doll says the same thing over and over and makes sense only if the little girl too is programed for the right questions. The activated cereal that is supposed to help a child lick every boy in the neighborhood tastes no different from any other, and the neighborhood bully still licks him.

What about the cynicism that is the outcome of such early disappointments? It is no real protection against gullibility. Like the "hinterlander" who has been burned many times, the child still falls for the new spiel of the next "snake oil" man. But he may develop a corrosive distrust of all adults, a distrust that does not help develop independent judgment. It undermines what the young child so badly needs: his trust in those around him so that he can learn and be guided by them. It furthers in the young child the much too early awareness of the seamy side of life against which he is still quite helpless, and it does not provide a foundation for development of his own sense of ethics.

II.
PLAYTIME—ATMOSPHERE AND SPACE

PLAYTIME

Much of the young child's time is spent in his own home. His family and his home-based activities are of major importance to his comfortable happy growth and development. Parents and children are often hard put to prepare or arrange for comfortable play space and an atmosphere in which the child can be constructively busy without too much distraction or bored by lack of guidance or the appropriate atmosphere to play.

"What shall I do? There's nothing to do." This plaint can be heard in almost any American home, almost any day, from youngsters of any age. And parents will view in disbelief their children's private toy stores piled in a corner or in a toy box. There are toys broken, and toys never played with. And, if the wail is loud enough, there will be a trip to the nearest supermarket. There the child will select still another piece of diversional equipment which, attractively attired in color and cellophane, will briefly catch his fancy and soon be added to the pile of dissatisfaction. And the plaint will resume. Why?

The pull and draw of the mechanical entertainer staring out into the living room is a heavy competitor of creative, imaginative, satisfactory play. It needs no thought or plan, it needs no adult assistance to set up or get started. Since in many families it is turned on most of the day, its presence is felt even if it is supposedly disregarded. Its background noises, the shooting, the yelling, the flickering of abruptly changing visual images intrude into every kind of quiet activity. If it is not the television, it may be the blare of radio music and noisy advertisements, or big brother's rock records. When all of these have quieted, there may be the washing machine, or at least a noisy refrigerator, a fan or the vacuum cleaner. The atmosphere is vibrating with noises and diversion, creating a climate of tension and underlying irritation that is the more disruptive because it is usually not consciously experienced as an irritant. Everyone seems accustomed to household noises, though we hear more and more about the part they play in the prevailing aura of tension and irritation. Such an atmosphere can hardly be conducive to the engrossed, quiet play of a young child.

But there are other factors operative in the child's inability to immerse himself in a satisfactory activity: The glut and onslaught of the "educational" toy attacks now ever-younger ages and is likely to undercut satisfactory activity if it comes too early or is inappropriate. These toys invade even the newborn's nursery. Children are now battered with stimulation from the very day they are born, long before their immature egos are able to defend themselves against stimuli which they are not yet able to master, to organize, or to store away. Such stimulation overwhelms them and leads to disorganization of orderly growth and development.

Even the unborn infant can already be entered into an educational system if his parents can afford it. There is now a piece of nursery equipment called the "Cognitive Crib." The advertisement for this is directed at mothers-to-be who can enroll their expected baby in a "learning environment" that provides the "Play Module" or the "Play Kit" of the month. A crib adapter provides for ever-changing stimulation of the tiny baby. The idea seems to be: Let him not waste precious time just lying in the crib gurgling and gazing around to discover the world at his own speed and readiness, or be cuddled and cooed to by those who love him. Push him to take notice and develop him into a genius. The experts (toy manufacturers) know what he needs. And the gullible parent will accept such an outrageous claim. The kit will provide mobiles with inter-changeable parts to force the baby to recognize colors and shapes whether he is neurologically ready for such awareness or not. There are live fish in a tank. And there are even mirrors on top of the crib to completely confuse an infant who is just beginning to learn about the real world; who is just beginning to develop eye–hand coordination and learn how to control his movements so he can touch something that is within his reach. Provided with this special crib attachment he can live in a three-ring circus and start life in complete confusion about what is real and what is image, and find that there is no restful place where he can escape this ever-changing imagery.

The very thought that "reading readiness" can be promoted by the time a small human being is a few months old will, of necessity, exert pressure on the parent. This in turn is bound to affect the child. If he does not voluntarily respond to the teaching equipment, the parents may begin to wonder whether there is something wrong with him. Maybe he needs more direct stimulation. Maybe, instead of using maternal playtime for responding to his cooing and for making him smile, he should be made to pay attention to the shapes and colors of his toys. It would be no pressure—it would be play—so say the promoters.

The new fashion in mobiles and infant toys may have good commercial value. Their developmental value has not been established and is questioned by many experts on early development.

The healthy young infant who is loved, played with, and has close physical contact with those who care for him soon begins to be interested in his environment and in what goes on. Stimulation comes naturally from the people around him. There will be plenty of shapes and colors to notice. There is a constantly changing world around him. If the environment is geared to the baby, and stimulation is gentle and appropriate to his age, and toys are simple and undemanding, he will respond increasingly as his abilities develop. If environmental demands become too great, he will try to fend them off. His techniques for this are few and primitive. He can press his eyes shut and he can cry. Sensitive parents who can respond to their children and discriminate distress signals may soon learn when his crying is not a demand for a bottle or a dry diaper, but an attempt to defend himself against too much stimulation, and they can tone down on the stimuli.

In a recent study, a British pediatrician warns against the demands on a baby's adaptability. She points out that the young infant's personality is still quite rigid and not conducive to quick adaptations. If they are forced on him, he will become depressed. Commercial advertisement tells the parent that he is depriving his child of valuable developmental opportunities by not providing all the educational equipment for him. The overzealous parent who accepts this premise may find himself with a very irritable baby who shows early disturbances in his daily functions—eating, digesting, sleeping, and gaining weight. He will not develop faster, as the promoters suggest—only more erratically.

But the fads for early cognitive development do not stop there. Baby books are pushed at the public, assuring parents that, "since the little one can now walk and talk, he is ready to learn to read." The very bedsheet tucked around the toddler at night can now become reading instructions. There are crib sheets on the market printed like books with pictures and words. Parents are admonished (by an industry that profits from new and startling inventions) to use the quiet, emotionally close time before the child goes to sleep to teach him the words printed on the sheet. And so to sleep and to nightmare land! What a quiet, relaxed bedtime hour! Do we really need to send a little child to sleep with a demanding task on his mind, as if he were an executive? Doctors tell us that ulcers, related to pressure and anxiety, are no longer rare in very young children.

Bedtime needs to be a quiet time for all of us, and even more so for the child. Any father knows that, if he picks the pre-bedtime hour for rough-housing with his children, the youngsters will be much too wound up to settle down for sleep. Bedtime has to be a time for slowing down. As Freud states: It is a time for withdrawing interest from the surroundings. It is a time for closeness between parent and child. Thus, the child will feel reassured about continuing protection and love. Nestled under old-fashioned non-reader sheets, the child could listen to a story. A quiet song or two or some conversation will facilitate sleep.

The promoters of the nursery gadgets tell us that there is no pressure intended—these are just play activities. They also say many parents do not know how to spend time with their young children. Parents will find teaching them a rewarding activity, important enough to assure the child some uninterrupted time with his elders. Whether this is a rewarding activity is very much to be questioned. It is not likely that it will bring parent and child closer together.

The current trend to make the parent into an extension schoolteacher or a pre-teacher does not enrich parent–child relationships. It only deprives the parent of the pleasures of "parenting" his children and turns the child into an orphan and a full-time student.

In their own homes children need parents, not teachers. To burden a mother, on top of all her other responsibilities, with the responsibility of turning her child into a budding genius does not make her a good teacher, nor a better mother. Not every child has the innate equipment for being a genius. He will assimilate academic knowledge when he reaches the necessary neurological, emotional, and intellectual maturity for such acquisition. To push such information at him before he is ready will result in his feeling pressured; in his much too early feeling of some shortcoming in himself; and quite likely in active or passive resistance against this external pressure. To put the onus of not having raised a genius on the parent will increase parental guilt to the detriment of the child.

A child's need for early development should not be pre-empted with cognitive tasks. Neither should the time parents have to spend with their children be pre-empted for structured teaching rather than be available for nurture.

Highly intellectualized parents may be pleased that

they have been given the tools for activities with their young children. Imagine the two-year-old who has never been played with, who does not know what a piggyback ride is, because his time has been occupied with being taught numbers and letters. By the time this child was two-and-a-half he needed therapy, primarily because he needed someone who loved him and could play with him on his own level.

What the intellectualized parent needs is probably some help in knowing how to respond to his offspring and establish the warm relationships all—parents and children—crave. Formal teaching is the function of the teacher and will be instituted at the appropriate time. Teaching and learning are important ingredients of the interaction between parent and child. But there are differences in what and how he learns in his relationship to his parents and that to his teachers. Relationship is an integral part of a child's learning and particularly important in his younger years. He learns initially only to please an adult. It will take many years before he realizes what value learning has to him.

Playtime should be a time of full absorption and creativity. The needs that a specific child has in his play are highly individual. They are as a rule not apparent to others, nor conscious to the child himself. In the right atmosphere, however, the child will gravitate toward the activities that satisfy his needs, that absorb him and give him pleasure. Constant stimulation by well-meaning but intrusive adults or ever-present mechanical noises are not conducive to the development of such an atmosphere. Real play activities are independent of expensive, complicated toys—educational or otherwise.

Play in an atmosphere where cognitive instruction takes such a prominent place is too often considered just a time filler. But play forms the basic matrix for a young child's learning. It continues to fulfill an important role in all our lives in relation to our continuous development and in the maintenance of our mental health. Play is neither diversional, nor should it be "structured" instruction. For the adult, play is a time of refueling, of draining off tension, of catharsis, of letting off steam. For the child it is a necessary ingredient for growth. It helps him master his environment by testing new approaches to everyday occurrences or finding problem solutions that can be accepted, modified, or discarded. It is an opportunity for relaxed learning in accordance with his own pace and inclination.

Overstimulation and glut of equipment lead to restlessness. All of us have seen young children become completely disorganized upon entering a toy department or even a too lavishly equipped nursery school. If the child lives at home in a miniature toy store, his attention will constantly vacillate between one thing and another, each thing looking tempting in turn, and none engaged in long enough to give satisfaction. Sooner or later the child becomes bored.

Boredom with his activities leads easily to aimless and /or destructive behavior, which in turn becomes subject to adult interruption. Parents as a rule expect the playing child to drop his activity promptly at their request and respond to their demands on him. Such frequent inter-ruption further undercuts absorption in the activity.

In group discussions parents frequently express their irritation with the playing child's delaying actions. "He's only playing; why shouldn't he come right away when he's called?" The parents will reconsider their own reac-tions when they become aware that they themselves may not respond promptly to a request made on them while they are reading, watching an interesting TV show, or otherwise engrossed in a pleasant activity.

Opportunities for quiet, uninterrupted playtime are a prerequisite for a child's even and successful develop-ment. This does not mean that the child should be per-mitted to dominate his surroundings with his activities, nor that the adults should submerge their own needs to cater to the child. Living together means the setting of priorities for mutual satisfaction and the development of respect for each other's needs. Children who are given more control over themselves or over others than they can manage are likely to become quite unsure and impos-sible to live with. By the same token, the child who is too much controlled by those around him will be just as dif-ficult. A mutually satisfactory arrangement has to include opportunity for protected playtimes for the child, times when he is neither called to pick up a dropped spoon, fetch the baby's diapers, or talk to Grandma on the phone.

We all have our own cycles; our own particular needs for active involvement with, or separation from, others; times of activities and times of rest, contemplation, and recuperation. In our pressured world these needs are seldom met for the adult. We are quite prone to outside interruptions with their frustrations and irritations. Such splintering of the natural rhythm of life comes early enough. Children should be afforded some protection of their needs. They should be permitted to let an activity run its course toward completion and be able to follow it with a quiet time.

I can almost hear the parents sigh, "I wish he had a quiet time. He's always on the go and underfoot." It might be well for such a parent to take stock for a moment and try to remember how anxious he becomes when the child is quiet, and how quickly *he* suggests another activity to prevent the youngster from getting into trouble.

I have seen a four-year-old standing at the window watching raindrops cruising down the pane, creating changing patterns of water drops and streaks and light reflections. He was engrossed and fascinated, but Mother became anxious about the quiet. She was sure the child was bored with staying indoors on a rainy day. In quick succession she suggested a half-dozen possible activities. The child turned. The spell was broken. He could not interpret an abruptly interrupted mood. He responded to the mother's subtle suggestion that he was bored and acted accordingly.

Because we live in such pressured times, the child's quiet, reflective moment is prone to cause anxiety. Reflection is equated with inactivity, inactivity with wasting time. This lack of acceptance of reflection, of the value of gathering in one's thought, and moods, and demands, gives rise to the feeling that children must not "waste time"; that their learning potential must be fully exploited during every moment of their waking hours. And, since a child must play, the play has to be consciously goal-directed toward his education. How fortunate for us—and for the child—that, as human beings, we are not perfect and have not been able to fully accomplish so ambitious a task as full exploitation.

Play does serve a child's education in the slow, meandering way of natural phenomena. The German writer Otto Ernst once said, in a delightful story about his children, *"Appleschnut"*: "The straight way is the shortest, but it is also the dullest."

The little stream winding its way through the woods does not get anywhere fast, but it is lovely and interesting. It invites lingering exploration of the small pools it forms. It leads to unexpected discoveries. If the line is straight and clear, the goal visible, even if far away, the temptation will be to reach it quickly, rather than to explore.

The same is true of children's learning. If given opportunity to meander at their own pace and inclination, they may make discoveries that no one would have thought of teaching them and that doubly impress them because they have been made on their own. Who knows what it was the little boy learned by watching the behavior of raindrops on a window? That the drops moved down and never up? That they changed shape as they joined others? One cannot say. No special "learning curve" may be developed for such acquisition of knowledge. But it is knowledge nevertheless—knowledge that for the child has an immediacy that no learning can have if it is limited, or prematurely pushed by adult goals and expectations regardless of the child's maturity and interest.

PLAY SPACE

The space provided for a child's play activities is as important as the atmosphere surrounding him and the equipment available to him. The setting in which the young child who is our main concern here lives and plays is primarily the home, a day-care center, or a nursery school. There will be more discussion of group settings in a later chapter. At this point we shall just consider space in the home.

All children, however big or small their homes, should have at least a corner set aside for safe, unencumbered play. One cannot expect parents in a small crowded apartment to enjoy stumbling over a cast-away doll or a forgotten truck. Nor can one expect children to remain engrossed in an activity when they play in the middle of the main traffic lane. If the setting provided for them allows for periods of uninterrupted play, they will be inclined to be satisfied with their activities. They will in turn also be more reasonable in their response to necessary limits regarding the number of toys in their corner as well as the end of playtime and some attempt to clear toys away.

Many a parent blessed with more lavish living space will be nonplussed by his child's own selection of play space. It seems that the space children most carefully stay away from is their own well-equipped room or the special playroom in the basement. The preferred place is often the kitchen, where mother is busy, or the living room, where "the action is." Young children want to be close to the people they love. Rather than engage in a useless battle and end with the child's disliking his own room as a place of isolation and separation, it may be wiser to consider a compromise. The clearly outlined play corner within view, adjacent to but not in the middle of other activities, may be the solution in most families. In this corner the child should have enough light to see what he is doing, a small table and chair where he can comfortably sit down, as well as some floor space. Even a young child will understand the give and take of compromise arrangements. "If you want to play in the kitchen, you have to stay over there so that I can go on with dinner." Or, "You may play in the living room and I will leave the kitchen door open. But you must not disturb Johnny while he is doing his homework." Thus, the child will learn to accept certain limitations, not as punishment, but as part of the structure of daily living; he will learn something about mutual consideration and feel accepted with his own needs by being able to consider the needs of others, besides being at ease with his own activity.

Where play space is not provided as part of an agreed-upon plan the family will find itself embroiled in a constant struggle. The child will begin to see himself as an intruder on other people's activities which rate so much higher than his own feeble attempts at being "busy." The usual reaction to feeling pushed away is to cling. This may initially just be the youngster's need for reassurance that he is still loved and part of the family. All too easily and too soon such behavior will be used by the child to taunt and annoy.

I remember a somewhat retarded three-year-old whose only satisfactory activity was running his little cars back and forth. The thick wall-to-wall carpeting in the home was very unsatisfactory for such play. So the child started to run his cars along the highly polished coffee table that was of a comfortable height for him and offered a most enticing surface. Mother, to protect her treasured table, put a quilt on it. The youngster then discovered the small area between the bathroom and the hall where he could use the marble threshold and a piece of exposed floor. This, of course, confined the activity to a tiny area and emphasized for the parents the limitations of their child. The repetitiveness of the activity and the sounds of the little cars going back and forth so within earshot got on their nerves and they tried to stop the child, who had no place left to do the one thing that provided interest and satisfaction to him. Because of the narrow confines of the space, there was also no possibility for him to develop the activity in any way beyond rolling the cars back and forth. The father, who was badly hurt by his son's limitations, became particularly irritated by this behavior. He started to bear down heavily on this activity. He soon noticed that the youngster would run for his little cars and the bathroom ledge as soon as the father entered the home. He kept glancing at his father as he made as much noise as possible with the cars. The father stated that it looked to him as if the child tried to provoke him, even though he knew he would eventually be spanked. It took much careful work with these parents to convince them that they were party to this provocative behavior because of the way they were further limiting an already limited child. The father's feeling that he had to have the authority to determine his child's behavior interfered with the recognition that he needed better techniques to help his child develop satisfactions that would assist him in outgrowing this repetitive behavior and undercut his need to provoke his father's attention in the only way in which he was successful.

The child's admission to a nursery school for handicapped children relieved some of the pressures on all parties involved. The parents had some respite from the child's behavior that was so irritating to them. The youngster was for a few hours in an unpressured situation where he had the space and opportunity to engage in play that was satisfactory to him, and where there was stimulation to move on to activities that helped him grow. The child's growth encouraged the parents to provide more adequate space for him at home, which in turn cut down on some of the irritation and warfare. The child did not suddenly become a brighter child, nor was the parents' hurt less real. But a compromise had been found. Parent and child could live more comfortably with each other, each in turn giving up some of an untenable position.

What is true for the struggle with a limited child is as true in relation to brighter children. They will be more resourceful, and will taunt, provoke, and in the end disregard restrictions if limits are unreasonable. But the bright child will most likely respond quickly and with pleasure to reasonable attempts at handling situations where horns are locked. But it has to be the adult who leads the way, because he has the maturity to work out a compromise and teach the child to negotiate. Negotiation, it should be noted, is not the same as bribery, since negotiation involves give and take.

III.
ACTIVITIES AND TOYS

THE HOME SCENE

Since home-based activities fill so much of the young child's time, they are of major importance to his comfortable, happy growth and development. Today's home is often hard pressed to meet the task of providing space and activities for such development. Provisions are made for children at ever-younger ages to be away from their own homes for periods of time. Some of such arrangements are unavoidable. Some are positive solutions to difficult reality conditions. But there are trends in the development of group care for young children that are regrettable because they are established for the wrong reasons, for monetary gains or to satisfy scientific considerations that do not always hold up. The young child's developmental and emotional needs are not always the prime movers in such planning. These aspects will be elaborated in the chapter on group experiences for young children.

But even the child who attends nursery school or a day-care center spends the greater part of his time in his own home. Home is where he first develops relationships and an image of himself. Home is where he belongs in the most literal sense of the word, and where he has or ought to have a stable base of operation. Home is where the young child spends most of those times during which routines and habits are established, and where he spends his weekends and enjoys his holidays. Home also is where his parents are and where he will be at times when he is ill and in need of close relationships and care.

Home activities are, therefore, of primary importance to the young child. Home is the place where his curiosity is stimulated and channeled, where he first enjoys being active, where constructive activities can be reenforced and destructive ones limited, where he learns to use time, to copy the activities of those around him, and to fit himself into a pattern of action and rest, where he learns to cope with the world around him and master his environment by acting, reacting, and testing.

But home is also the place where he will get underfoot, since he prefers to be where others are and where he might easily get into trouble in today's home with its fascinating and often dangerous gadgets that are a lure to inquisitive, busy little hands and which have not been installed with the young child in mind. The house that is full of "touch-me-nots," such as low-sitting flowerpots, heavy, precariously positioned art objects or floor lamps, or low-hanging table cloths presents too many inviting child traps.

To teach the child to live safely in his home, to learn to respect mother's precious violets and daddy's heavy ashtrays and engage in activities that do not leave the house in a shambles, will take involvement and time on part of the adults. With a crawler or a toddler at the house it is a good idea to temporarily reduce the number of touch-me-nots and teach the child quietly and patiently what he may handle and what he must leave alone. The best antidote against investigation of those things that could bring danger to him is to limit the number of child traps and offer him attractive activities that suit his age and interest.

It does take time and imagination to provide opportunities for a young child in his own home for constructive, absorbing activities that will not constantly interfere with the activities of others. It takes empathy with the child that stems from love for him. The parent who feels he or she is too busy or too tired to spend this time will find that he spends endless periods running after a toddler in trouble, scolding, cleaning up, preventing near-disasters, and handling a cross, resisting child. The training of a child to respect limits, the introduction and setting-up of pleasurable activities, will indeed take a block of time. Such time given cheerfully before it is demanded or forced is an investment that pays dividends.

These dividends will be a satisfied child who repays the parent by developing well, by learning, and by creating his own ideas and interests. He will repay by his ability to cooperate and thus will cut down on time that the adult would have to spend in settling and correcting disasters.

The few minutes Mother will spend to introduce her toddler to the kitchen equipment he may use—the time she spends to set up a corner for play with water or sits down to show him how to make a cookie dough without dusting the whole kitchen with flour and how to handle the cookie cutter—will free her to go on with her own work with just an eye on the playing child. If she keeps sporadic attention on him, talks to him, engages in a song, responds to his imagery, or helps him over a snag in his activity and warns him off if he tries to explore the firmness of limits set, they may both have a busy time without strain and with a closeness that is as satisfactory to the mother as it is to the child. Such an experience is growth promoting, even if it is less pointedly "educational" than the hours spent passively watching even the best TV program.

Much good, creative home play equipment is quite inexpensive and not necessarily found in toy departments. The listings of activities and toys in this chapter are not meant to be either complete or original. They simply provide suggestions which can be parent savers when demands are made at times when ideas have dried up, when tempers are flaring, when a special holiday comes around, or when it has been raining all week.

POTS AND PANS

The kitchen cabinet, with its pots, pans, lids, and wooden spoons, is heaven for the crawler and the toddler, as every mother knows. The wise mother, rather than fight the child's inclination, will designate one cabinet or shelf for his use. He will soon learn to respect what is off limits if he has free range in a particular area within his reach. Having interesting playthings while close to Mother will help him to acquire a beginning understanding of "Yes" and "No" that will provide a base for the start of discipline and internalized controls. Mother can relax about her youngster's whereabouts, and at the same time protect her best kitchen equipment from serving as noisemakers or teethers.

As he gets a little older, the home furnishes additional interesting pieces of equipment for busy hands and minds.

WATER PLAY

This can provide endless enjoyment and does not have to get out of hand if grounu rules are set ahead of time. The kitchen sink before which the child teeters on a chair and from which he is moved whenever the sink is needed for other purposes is not the best place for this. A large pan partially filled with tepid water and set on a low table or on a piece of plastic on the floor out of the way will be less messy and more satisfactory. A piece of plastic or a plastic apron can be put on the child to prevent his being soaked. Any old, spouted, and unbreakable pot (a coffeepot or small teakettle) makes an intriguing toy and can keep a large range of ages busy and happy. The younger child will be content with just filling and pouring, while older ones will find many variations to the game. A tea strainer, a ladle, a funnel, plastic bottles with wide or narrow mouth, boats, floating toys, cups, doll dishes can be added. Again, the younger the child, the bigger should be the pan and the lower the water level. Mother could show him briefly how to fill the pot and how to pour. She will be wise to watch him in the beginning to warn him against willful spills as soon as he starts to splash. Once he has found out how much fun it is to make a mess he may be out of control. If he does get over enthusiastic, it is better to put the things away quietly and tell him that there will be another chance soon. The mother may restate that the water has to stay in the pan when he is playing, without emphasizing that he is being punished. He will get the idea without being too upset and without needing to test Mother's endurance too often. To keep him away from an enjoyable experience because he overexperimented the first time will not teach him to handle this elusive liquid more competently, but it will deprive him of a constructive experience. What he learns by managing water in the big pan can help him later when he wants to learn to pour his own milk or juice.

As the child gets older, he will enjoy a mild soapy solution to squish, to bathe a doll, to wash toys or doll clothes, to wash a real hankie, a washcloth, a dishrag, or his own socks. This may give him a feeling of real accomplishment. If a mild soap is used rather than a detergent he might be given a bubble pipe to blow soap bubbles. (It is quite a skill to learn to blow instead of sucking on a pipe.)

As he learns to handle water carefully, he could be shown how to mix water and flour to make dough. Mixing flour and water is an entrancing activity for many ages. Careful preparation for this activity will insure its success. This, again, will take a little time. Newspaper or a piece of plastic under the table will protect the kitchen floor. The child should be seated comfortably, preferably at a small chair and table set. To have a young child kneel on a full-sized kitchen chair and try to reach the kitchen table is inviting trouble. If he has to balance while handling elusive materials he is bound to spill, drop things, or fall off the chair. To mix flour and water he should have two bowls, one partially filled with the flour, one empty, a small pitcher partially filled with water, a dry spoon in the flour so that he can transfer small amounts of flour to the empty bowl, and a wooden spoon with which to mix the flour with the water which he is learning to pour slowly and carefully in small amounts into the flour. It is important that bowls and pitcher are only partially filled for easier handling. To give a child the already partially mixed ingredients will be neater but will take away from the real fun and learning potential of this activity. The transferring of ingredients and observing their behavior is half the fun. To see the batter thicken as more flour is added and thinning out when water is poured in provides the interest. As the child gains in skill he might enjoy the use of a hand eggbeater for mixing. Once he has mastered this part of the activity he might like to prepare his own cocoa and follow directions for proportions of ingredients.

Initially, the mixing itself is the activity. Only later will the child be able to do something with the batter. He can then learn to make dough. As he manipulates it with clean hands and adds a little sugar and shortening, and uses a rolling pin and cookie cutters, he will be intrigued with the fact that the end result of his activity can be baked and eaten.

If the batter is mixed with a little salt to retard spoilage, the child can prepare his own play dough to form figurines, dishes, or beads that can be painted or shellacked. A thinner batter can be boiled to make an inexpensive paste or as a base for fingerpaints. Food coloring added will make for brilliant colors for this activity. Fingerpaints can be used then on large sheets of inexpensive newsprint. This can be hung to dry on laundry hooks and later used to make lovely covers for boxes or books, or just pictures to hang on the wall.

Pouring can be enjoyed with dry ingredients as well. Farina, for instance, lends itself quite well to this. It can be poured through a strainer into a bowl or through a larger funnel into a bottle. If it is mixed with rice or lentils the child will watch with fascination how the finer farina goes through the strainer while the rice or lentils stay in it. For this activity he ought to have three bowls: one for the mixture, one into which he can strain the farina, and one in which to discard the coarser grains. He can remix and restrain for a long time.

OTHER KITCHEN AND HOME SUPPLIES

Other inexpensive activities are also found right in the kitchen cabinets or around the house. Macaroni makes lovely necklaces, bracelets, a boy's Indian hairband or a princess's diadem, or Christmas tree decorations if strung on string. They can be covered, painted, or shellacked. Smaller, flatter noodles can be sprinkled on paste blobs on paper to make designs or attractive wrappings, or coverings for gift boxes.

BEANBAGS AND OTHER TOYS TO THROW

All children enjoy throwing things. This can be hazardous in doors, but activities that are prompted by the child's physical or emotional needs cannot be simply ignored or forbidden. It is always better to neutralize negative aspects of an activity and provide adequate substitutes. Beanbags, sponge rubber balls, and whiffle balls are fairly nondestructive. Areas where throwing with these toys is permissible can be delineated. A large box makes a beautiful target and clarifies an area. A somewhat older child will enjoy sailing paper plates at a target, or playing catch with them with someone else. Straws can be used as arrows to provide inexpensive, nondangerous fun.

GROWING THINGS

One of the most fascinating activities for a young child is to make things grow. Many of the ingredients can come right out of the kitchen supplies. One of the simplest and quite impressive results can be achieved with dry beans and lentils. These can be grown on damp cotton so that the child can observe the swelling and bursting of the seed, the breakthrough of the root as it is shooting downward, and the young green sprouts growing upwards. Preparations for this activity are simple. A layer of absorbent cotton on a shallow dish (an old saucer will do) is moistened thoroughly, and the beans or lentils are sprinkled on the surface. The cotton is kept moist by adding water as it is absorbed by the seeds or evaporates. Roots will appear within a few days and the green shoots come soon after. Plants can be kept as they are or planted in a flowerpot, cotton and all. Bird seed, too, might be used in the same way.

A fascinating hanging vine can be grown from a sweet potato. A piece of the potato that has a number of "eyes" is cut off. It can be kept on wet cotton like the beans or suspended with toothpicks on the top of a small glass of water. The cut surface of the potato has to touch the water level, which has to be maintained so the potato won't dry. It too can eventually be planted in a clay pot. Plants from seeds of lemons, oranges, or grapefruits, planted in soil in small clay pots, will come up within five to six weeks. They have to be watered but not drowned and make lovely plants that can grow even in the house into trees if well tended. While these activities are well within the ability of a young child, the youngster will need adult assistance to insure success. Keeping cotton and soil moist without drowning the plants or forgetting all about them until they have dried up needs adult reminders and supervision. The end product is well worth the effort.

BOXES

Boxes in all sizes and shapes provide an almost endless variety of play equipment for all ages. The size of the box is often in inverse ratio to the size of the child. The smaller the child, the bigger the box. The large supermarket variety makes a lovely hiding place for the toddler to crawl into, and to throw things in and out of, though he will also like a small box with a lid which he can open and close. Older children may cover a big box with cutouts or their own fingerpaintings and use them as toy chests. They can use them to build houses, trains, tunnels, garages, stores, and can probably think of a dozen more uses. Smaller boxes can be transformed into doll beds and other furniture. Covered with pretty paper they can be turned into gift boxes, receptacles for pencils, string, etc., etc.

MAGAZINES

Almost any home has an assortment of old magazines, Christmas cards, or picture postcards. The very small child loves to tear paper and can be best prevented from getting at the family's treasured books by being given a small store of discarded magazines. Seated on the floor with a wastebasket at his side, he can have a blissful time tearing and throwing the scraps into the basket. A rug or a piece of plastic will catch the inevitable "fallout" to make cleaning up easier; it will also protect the child if the floor is rough or cold. As he gets older he can be shown how to cut with blunt scissors. He will begin to see the outline of a picture and gradually learn to cut around it. He can make scrapbooks by pasting the pictures on large sheets which can be stapled into books. He might make up his own stories to fit the pictures, and Mother or big sister can write the stories down for him. It does not matter if, initially, the stories don't hold together too well. He will develop awareness and a knack.

As the child cuts or tears papers, a wastebasket should always be part of the scene, and the discarding of the scraps should be part of the activity.

PARTICIPATION IN HOME CHORES

Young children love to participate in everything those around them engage in. While Mother does not always appreciate such assistance since it slows her down, her offspring does. The young child's assistance may be somewhat detrimental to the quality of her housekeeping, but it may considerably improve the quality of child rearing. Even the three- and four-year-old can be assigned some simple regular chores. While the adults may feel that the most appropriate chore for him would be to keep his toys picked up, they will find that this is the chore the child himself rates lowest. He will want a more "grown-up" chore. Keeping his toys straightened and put away should, of course, be part of his assignment. He will need help with this even if he seems old enough and quite capable of doing it by himself. But he can also empty wastebaskets and ashtrays, dust low surfaces, put laundry in the hamper, sort clean laundry, set the table, and perform probably another half-dozen chores dependent on the particular needs of the household. With all the emphasis on early learning many of these chores will teach him matching, counting, sequencing, etc., in a very "relevant" way. I know of a three-year-old who learned to count and to recognize and name colors because her job was to count out candy for herself and her eight siblings.

The pre-schooler loves to be involved in cooking, and there is quite a variety of tasks he can easily perform if given the right tools and instruction. He can help make jello or puddings. Comfortably positioned at a small table with newspaper underneath to catch what might drop, he can scrape potatoes or carrots with a scraper (scraping away from his body). He can certainly spread his own sandwich for lunch with jam or peanut butter if a limited amount is put in a small bowl and he is given a dull knife. This will teach him to recognize a shape and fill in an outline with more immediacy than the dull interminable outlines of squares offered now even to the pre-schooler in nursery school for "reading readiness" training. Since the slice of bread is three-dimensional he will soon know whether he is staying within the "outline" or going beyond the edges.

With the experience he has gathered from his water play, he should be able to pour his own milk or juice from a small pitcher or fill the water glasses for everyone at the table. Thus, he can apply what he has learned of the propensities of liquid and the relationship between a small glass and a larger pitcher. He can learn something about the relationship of the size of the serving dish, the serving spoon, his plate, and his appetite if permitted to dish out his own supper. He will, as with most practical tasks, also get a lesson in social adjustment. He will learn that his own appetite is not the only concern as he serves himself. There are others to be served and they, like him, have a claim on a favorite dish. This is important learning.

He will make a mess? Very likely, at first. But he also made a mess when he first learned to feed himself. With a little help, a lot of praise, and some controls he learned to manage then and he will learn to manage now. The investment of time by the adult who teaches him will mean time saved in the long run. His pleasure in mastery of complicated processes and his feeling of being a contributing member of his family will go a long way in setting patterns of cooperation and love and beginning social awareness, and help him develop into a social being.

PETS

Pets are the delight of almost all children. They provide endless joy, stimulation, and emotional attachment for the child. Their care teaches the child responsibility for another living being and attention to the needs of someone more helpless than himself. However, pets should be in the household only if the adults too enjoy them and are willing and able to take much responsibility for their care and protection. The living pet is a source of deep enjoyment to the child. But pets do die at times even with the best of care. The adults have to be prepared to help a child with the unhappiness and disappointment caused by such an experience. To quickly replace a dead kitten with a substitute means missing the significance of the experience and assuming a shallowness of attachment. If the dead kitten can be exchanged so quickly, the child might easily wonder whether he, too, is exchangeable. The grieving child needs recognition of his feeling of loss and permission to be sad. He needs comforting before he is promised a replacement.

To provide a child with a pet in a city apartment may present some problems because of available space or lease restrictions. However, gerbils or similar small pets may be quite acceptable. Even fish can be fun. I once possessed a blue Beta which made a lovely splash of color and movement in a small apartment. After a few weeks the fish would come to the surface of the tank when I approached and nibble his food from my finger. While this is not the same as holding a cuddly kitten or romping with a puppy, it can provide a source of interest and fun for a child.

IMAGINATIVE PLAY

The whole area of imaginative play is an important one, though it is sadly neglected in our automated, mechanistic times. A recent article by a psychologist discussed the importance of imagination and imaginative play for young children to enable them to develop and learn. It sounded almost as if this were a new discovery; and, as a true exponent of our times, the writer felt that anything that could be taught should be and recommended that, since imagination was so important to children, it should be *taught* in their group settings. Nothing would kill imagination faster than an attempt to teach it. Imaginative play needs to be encouraged, however, and opportunity for its development needs to be provided for children in their homes as well as in the groups they attend.

Since the home is the first "developmental laboratory" for the child, his imagination should find ample nutrition there. Many parents find it quite easy to participate in their children's imaginative play activities while they go along with their own activities and chores.

They can respond to the "postman" or the "delivery man" as he comes to the house with his deliveries. They can visit with a "neighbor" or "taste" the dollhouse stew, and even assign some actual chores as part of a child's role playing. "Oh, Mrs. Smith, you make such marvelous stew, nobody washes potatoes as well as you do. Would you now . . ." or sending "Mr. Mac" upstairs to inspect the bathroom for leaks and be good enough to bring the laundry down, or have Danny apprenticed to his father as he repairs and paints a piece of furniture. The everyday things around the house, from discarded clothing to discarded equipment, provide imaginative stimulation and thus enrichment of a child and his personality. Even the most imaginative TV program will not promote a child's imagination to the same degree. It is somebody else's imagination that is presented to the passively viewing child, though, in a household where imagination is given house room and TV time is limited, the child may pick up ideas for his own play activities from some enjoyable show he sees.

Busy mothers may prefer self-development skills for their child and want to spend less time on involvement with his play. Since television teaches letters and numbers without human involvement, it may be considered a "mother saver." And so we may encounter the three-year-old who can count to twenty before he is able to pull his socks on his feet or his shirt over his head. He keeps Mother busy doing things for him that he could have learned and done for himself, while his ability to count could be acquired at almost any time of his life.

If mothers take stock, they will find that they do spend time with their children one way or another. They do it either by having some enjoyable playtime and time when they are teaching the child skills of daily living and developing mutual love and concern. Or they do it settling fights, cleaning up mishaps, wearing a groove in the rug trying to keep junior in bed, scolding and punishing —not a profitable time for either child or parent. The only skill the youngster is acquiring is that of manipulating the adult and forcing attention. Children fight against being abandoned, however subtle the abandonment. They are quite skilled in making adults take notice. Even a spanking is preferred to going unnoticed. Time offered cheerfully before it is demanded is an appreciated gift that is enjoyed, constructive, and, as a rule, not as protracted as forced attention.

COMMERCIAL TOYS

The vehicle for a child's play is not only home equipment, but to a large degree the toy. There is an abundance of good toys on the market. At the risk of being obvious I want to restate: The marks of the good toy are that it is attractive, safe, sturdy, imaginative, and versatile and that it can be managed without a college degree in engineering or mechanics.

For home use, toys should be carefully selected to meet the needs and inclination of the particular child or sibling group for whom they are chosen. They should be limited in number and fit the particular family's pocketbook. Toys out of keeping with the family's budget will, in case of damage or loss, draw reactions that are out of proportion to the situation. Children certainly should learn to care for their toys. If the need to care for them is dictated by the price tag rather than by the wish to establish good habits, the pleasure and freedom in the use of the toy will be considerably diminished.

The "educational" toy (and which toy today is not designated "educational" by its promoters?) is designed for self-service learning of the young. It can be quite attractive and useful. However, because of the high pressure promotion of some educational toys, a word of caution may be in order. It is not the value of the good toy that needs to be questioned. However, one needs to guard carefully against commercial exploitation of children and their requirements, as well as against exploitation of bewildered parents who want to do an adequate job and provide their offspring with the best they can afford.

Basic, simple toys have survived many centuries and have joyfully engaged countless generations of children because of their versatility and their responsiveness to basic needs, to the stage of maturity, and to the imagination of many different individuals who develop at their own speed.

Any attempt to list these veterans of the toy family will be fraught with omissions, but let's try anyhow.

There are *balls* and *building blocks* in many shapes and sizes, *small buildings* to create towns and cities and farms. There are *animals* of diverse sizes and materials. There are *dolls* and *hand puppets* and *puppets on strings*. There are *doll furniture* and *doll dishes*. There are *puzzles* simple and complicated. There are *pull toys* and *wagons*. And there are *beads*. Of a somewhat later vintage, but as beloved and serviceable are: *trains* and *cars* and *trucks* and *boats* and *planes*—little editions for the youngster who carries them in his pocket, bigger ones for floor play, and very large ones that will transport the child. There is the much beloved *tricycle* or *bicycle*. And there are *books* and *books* and *books* for all ages and stages of interest and sophistication. Books to look at and books for someone to read to the child. And there is the sturdy, simple *record player* that can be manipulated by even a young child.

There is the *Tinkertoy* and all its variations, and there are *magnets.*

Then there are playthings with which to create. In this category belong all the things to which the child needs some introduction to manage. This should not mean that the youngster is shown what to do or must observe an adult at play. He only needs to learn the techniques of handling the material. In this category belong:

PLAY DOUGH

This needs little introduction beyond showing the child that the material ought to be kept on a board or a place mat to confine the mess. He will take to the kneading and squeezing and rolling all by himself. And he will discover soon that some of the shapes are representative. Then he will copy himself or another child playing with him.

Clay and *plasticine* are less popular at present, though they too have marvelous properties and give much pleasure.

Big crayons and felt-tipped markers are important basic play materials and entrance with their vivid colors. Young children need to be given large sheets of paper to draw on. The child may be little but his motions are large and not yet very well controlled. He will probably prefer to work on the floor if it is not carpeted. If it is, a large piece of plywood or composition wood makes a good hard surface.

Paints will need a bit more introduction, and initially the child should work under some supervision. Small watercolor sets and small brushes are very unsatisfactory for the young child. Poster paints in jars, large brushes, and large sheets of paper will be highly satisfactory. If an easel is used it should be stable. Otherwise, one might protect a wall with large sheets of newspaper taped on with masking tape and tape the child's paper to this surface. The floor can also be protected with newspaper or plastic. The child should never use a full jar of paint since this invites spills and splashes. The paint jars should be positioned on a small table or stool, on the right hand side of the child who is right handed, on the left for the left-handed one. He needs to be shown just how to dip and wipe the brush to get the right amount of paint. And after he has mastered this technique he needs to be left alone to his own blossoming creative urge.

Wood, tools, and nails will entrance both boys and girls. The tools should be sturdy. No one can hammer a nail into a piece of wood with a lightweight hammer or cut it with a dull saw. But the child who plays with such material will need careful instruction in its use and an adult nearby for a long time to prevent accidents.

GAMES

We must not neglect the array of games available on the market. They, like any toy or activity, have to be chosen according to their value for a particular child or group of children. Age makes a difference; so does an adult available to help the youngster understand and maintain rules and monitor the activity. Young children do not easily accommodate to game structure, even if they do understand it. Losing comes very hard for many, and cheating quite easy. Children love to have an adult play with them. It makes losing a bit easier and winning more fun. Most adults enjoy a game session with their children.

The available selection is almost endless. Lottos, simple or more complicated; simple card games and board games; and, for the somewhat older child, checkers or Chinese checkers—this is a beginning list.

OUTDOOR ACTIVITIES

Many outdoor activities need no special equipment. The healthy, non-TV-addicted pre-schooler loves to be out of doors. Just running, rolling down a grassy slope, picking up colored pebbles, or collecting the many things offered by nature (from leaves to chestnuts to bugs) will keep him happy. Digging in soil or sand with a spoon or a shovel is one of a young child's favorite activities. A bucket or a small truck which he can fill will add to the enjoyment. A jar and a small net to catch minnows if he lives close to the water is also great fun for the young child.

Wagons and tricycles have already been mentioned. Roller skates and ice skates and sleds should be added to the list. Again, the list can be extended depending on available safe outdoor play space and the size of the family wallet. Even with a pint-size backyard and a small coin purse many families do provide a sandbox, a small plastic pool, or a slide or a swing. Old car tires have endless uses, doubling as swings, as targets for throwing, etc.

The young child can be introduced to outdoor games when there is a group or an adult or an older child at hand to provide some leadership and see that a few basic rules are observed. Otherwise, games will quickly deteriorate into fights. Tag and hide-and-seek with all their variations can be fun once the child understands simple game structure and can adhere to it. He will probably pick up many games if he lives in a neighborhood where he can observe and join older children.

Competetive sports are not very suitable for young children. It is an error to think that they will adjust more easily to a competitive world if they are pushed into competition early. They may become just more vulnerable and try to cover up by overaggressiveness. But there are many kinds of individual sports where a child can attain individual competence rather than trying to become more competent than others. Skating, bicycling, various running and ball games that do not depend too strictly on teams or structure can be quite satisfactory to the preschooler and to younger children. Team spirit necessary for competitive group games and sports is acquired slowly and presupposes a certain amount of maturity.

THE RAINY DAY OR SICK-IN-BED BOX

For the child who is confined to the house by illness or by a stretch of bad weather, all familiar activities will eventually pall. It is a good idea to have a box stored away with toys or activities that are brought out only on such occasions. In such a box can be a few new things, as well as some old ones which the child has previously enjoyed but discarded. A bed table can easily be constructed for the bed-bound youngster by cutting a space for his legs in a heavy, large box. The blanket can be protected by a piece of plastic. A wastebasket next to the bed will catch debris. A new box of crayons or felt-tipped markers may seem like a brand-new toy. Things to cut out, like paper dolls or animals, will keep the youngster busy not only with cutting but by providing him with the basics for some phantasy and role play. Other supplies will depend on the child's current limitations, and on the parent's knowledge of what his child enjoys or has wished for. Even a live fish in a bowl can keep a feverish, tired child quietly engaged for quite a while.

TOYS TO BE VIEWED WITH SUSPICION

The supply of good, serviceable toys is plentiful, but there is an array of toys on the market that should be viewed with a good deal of reservation. These creations too may have their day, but it will probably be a short one.

The self-limiting toy is not a good toy, however attractive the packaging or advertising. The toy that will perform and entertain independently may be amusing for a while but has very limited play value.

In this category belong the complicated, mechanical toy creations like dancing dolls or robots that shoot. These may be more satisfactory to the giver than to the receiver.

They may indeed delight the child at first. Quite soon, however, the repetitiveness of the toy's action palls on the child, the parts get lost, or the whole thing breaks down. Such toys do not engage a child's sustained interest and do not challenge him. They fail him, however educational may be their intent.

Another example of the self-limiting toy is the pre-packaged kit. Its clearly specified activities are frequently quite deadening. However interesting the original activity may be, in the kit there is a narrow, pre-set goal. The exact kinds and amounts of pre-cut, pre-shaped pieces to complete a specific task, and a picture of what the finished product will look like are provided. There are directions to be followed. The loss of, or damage to, a piece renders the kit useless. Since the child has already been shown what the end product should look like, chances that he will try to use what is left to create something different are slim. A set goal that cannot be reached creates frustration. It takes a fairly mature or specially gifted child to find frustration a challenge. Most children will dissolve in tears and throw the expensive half-used kit onto the heap of other half-used toys. If completed, the toy has "self-destructed." Kits do not invite imaginative uses, variation, and experimentation. Kits for leather-work (read: belts, billfolds) weaving (read: potholders or belts again), etc., are expensive. When the scant raw material is used up, there are no refills available, or it seems too troublesome to locate a source. Even if the child's interest has been aroused, he cannot invent new uses for the gadgets. There is only the possibility to buy another kit complete with frames, spools, etc., to add to the clutter in the nursery.

Another quite distressing example of uncreative activity that deadens a child's natural inclination and gifts is the much beloved *coloring book.* It is supposed to engage the child in an independent activity that is "good for him," teaches him to draw, and prepares him for writing by training him in recognizing outlines and developing fine muscle control. *De facto,* it does none of these. As an independent activity it is very attractive to the adult. (There is considerable interest in developing independence early in children. We will discuss the pros and cons as well as the timing of this aspect of child rearing when we talk about relationships and their value.) Filling in of pre-prepared outlines in a paintbook does not teach drawing. The purely mechanical task leaves the child emotionally quite uninvolved in his activity.

The child learns to draw and paint basically the same way he learns other things: by neurological readiness, by experimenting, by observing and repeating accidental successes. He learns to talk by playing with his speech equipment and responding to his own and other sounds in his environment. He learns to walk by crawling and falling, by discovering that he can determine the direction in which he wants to propel himself. And he will learn to draw by random scribbling and emulating his own accidental successes and by a response that greets his creations with pleasure.

From the coloring book, just as from the much overused school workbook, he acquires clichés that will interfere with the keenness of his observations and the development of his innate abilities. A recent study (*But What's Wrong with Coloring Books?*, March 1972, Connecticut Art Education Assn.) discusses the extremely restrictive effect of these introductions to art for children. The fact that many children love coloring books does not make this equipment any more valuable. Children like repetitive activities. They constitute a part of their practice toward a goal. But there should be a possible goal. The coloring book is a dead end. It may play into an undesirable compulsive streak or into the need for easy success, when early criticism has made him fearful of failure.

The technical difficulties of managing a coloring book are inclined to restrict the child, rather than encourage freedom of movement and coordination. The sheets and figures are small. The child's hands and half of his attention will be engaged in keeping the book flat and prevent it from falling shut. Large sheets of plain paper and big crayons or colorful thick-tipped markers will entrance the child and encourage experimentation. He will be absorbed in the activity rather than distracted by technical problems, and the finished product will satisfy him.

THE DEATH RATE OF TOYS

It is not surprising that the death rate of toys and activities in our country is enormous. The reason for this is partly that toys, like washing machines and cars, have built-in obsolescence. There is also the glut of toys and play equipment which encourages the discarding of still very satisfactory toys in order to provide the newest and most advanced one. But there is also the modern push for "instant maturity."

While one occasionally will want to give a child a toy that he will outgrow in a brief period of time, this should not be the rule. Only the toy that can be used over and over stimulates imagination and exploration and offers a diversity of use. When the use of a particular toy over a long period of time is equated with lack of development, parents and children can easily be made to feel that they are not "with it" if toys are not replaced in quick succession with what is the latest advance or refinement in children's "enjoyable learning equipment." While this, of course, is commercially desirable, it is costly to the parents but also to the child who is deprived of the opportunity to develop at his own speed and to be deeply absorbed in an activity—and who is being made to feel that not having the latest edition of a certain toy is a serious deprivation.

Research findings regarding children, their stages of development, and ways to measure this development based on the activities they prefer and the toys they use are highly popularized and presented to parents often before they have been fully documented and evaluated. Parents are given the impression that maturity can be hastened by providing the right kind of toy, and by removing the one he has supposedly outgrown.

Under these circumstances, the tricycle is outgrown almost before the child has really mastered the necessary balance and coordination to stay on and make it move.

He and his parents are shamed into providing a regular bike with training wheels which in turn soon have to be removed. And, while Europe's ten-year-olds still enjoy vigorous activity on the scooter (not the motorized one), we here are pushing the minibike for his contemporaries, to promote early competitiveness rather than healthy physical activity. (The real danger and the unhealthy tension that are created for the young rider are argued away.)

Doll play and sand play are crossed off the list of appropriate activities very early. If one watches older children at the beach, where they are unself-conscious and surrounded by sand, one realizes how much they still enjoy this pliable play material and how imaginative their creations can be.

As far as doll play goes, the simple doll meant for cuddling and for playing house is hard to come by. In the modern mechanical creations the mechanism likely as not predetermines the use of the doll. Hair that grows, a record in the belly, a mechanism to make the doll dance may make the doll a "showpiece" as advertised, but not an object for loving, mothering, and role play. Precocious sophistication is pushed in the doll who represents a teenager, complete with boyfriend and fur jacket. Today's doll often comes already equipped with a name so that the child does not even have the pleasure and personalized relationship of finding the name that she herself wants to give the doll.

Even reading, promoted with such verve for the preschooler, is frowned upon early as an activity if it cuts down on the young boy's interest in competing on the ball field. Reading, it would seem, is considered just a necessary skill of recognizing words rather than a satisfactory activity in its own right that can provide pleasure and information and open up a whole fascinating world for the child. It is pushed much too soon and devalued much too early.

Parental pride in a child's fast development and seeming sophistication falls in with this rush and results in early acquired and quickly discarded skills. This leaves the child floundering for lack of direction and for want of absorbing activities. If activities are presented as skills and as steps in an endless ladder of diversions, interest is bound to wane as soon as the skill is halfway mastered, and long before application of the skills supplies any real satisfaction or any end products.

Under environmental pressure, a child may discard activities that still serve a developmental purpose for him. Thus, he will lose out not only on pleasure, but on practice of developmental skills and on completion of a natural process. Such children are likely to grow an outer crust of pseudosophistication which they cannot really maintain, but which will insulate them against age-appropriate learning.

I know of a five-year-old who was under severe pressure to meet his parents' great expectations of him as a "big boy." The parents were urged to enter him in a camp to give him contemporary companionship and relaxed, age-appropriate activities. The youngster practically insulated himself for a long time against the fun at camp.

When, on his entrance, the counselor took him around to show him the campsite and the prospective activities, he defended himself with a bored attitude. Sheep and rabbits, oh, he had seen them before. Horses—yeah, he knew about horses and wasn't interested in riding one. Walks in the woods or swimming—he had had all that. It took this poor youngster many days to enter in the vigorous play and fun with the other children when they were swimming, sawing down a tree to make a bridge, finding out that they could reach the dining room by walking through a brook, and just generally having fun.

The "there is nothing to do" syndrome is a logical sequence to this approach to activities. The child who counters the suggestion that he might try painting or leatherwork with: "Oh, I know all about this, I had painting in school," or, "We did leatherwork at camp," is sadly reminiscent of an old joke. It seems there was an aunt at a loss as to what to give her nephew for his birthday. When a book was suggested her answer was: "A book he has already." And so the home gets glutted with play equipment that is too quickly outgrown and too expensive to throw away—and peopled with children who want to be busy rather than interested and need ever-changing mechanical stimulation to be so.

IV.
GROUPS FOR YOUNG CHILDREN

Groups for young children have become a necessity in our current culture. Today's individual home can rarely offer the young the social experiences they need to develop into well-rounded social beings who can enjoy social situations and deal with their complications. In spite of this need, which is quite general, the existing preschools cater to a large degree to specialized groups and are designed more often to meet adult requests than the requirements of the pre-school population as a whole.

The financially affluent have no difficulty arranging for group experiences for their offspring to meet the child's or their own wishes. Cooperative nursery schools are available to serve those children whose mothers share in the care of the children to defray the financial outlay. Special interest groups, like religious organizations and agencies for the retarded or otherwise handicapped children, meet specialized needs of a particular clientele and provide for a sliding tuition scale. Day-care centers care for the children of working mothers at greatly reduced costs to the parents.

This leaves large groups of young children unserved. These are children whose families have neither the funds to pay nor the time to barter for service. They are children who do not have the clearly focused need for supervision or specialized care. Their needs are the generalized needs of young children for social contacts and for compensatory experiences that their own homes cannot provide.

Unfortunately, group care for the pre-school–age child of the less affluent has become entangled in a number of side issues of vested interests, political and otherwise. This is drawing attention from the real issue and obscures needs, intentions, and realistic goals of group program for this age.

Discussion here will be limited to the needs and benefits of group experiences for the pre-schooler (aged about three to five) without consideration of side issues. Attention will be drawn also to the pitfalls and dangers of efforts to use the educational and developmental requirements of children to build big industrial, financially highly remunerative ventures.

BASIC NEEDS

Of course, many young children are perfectly well provided with desirable social and other opportunities within their own homes. But the difficulty of meeting some of the young child's basic needs in his natural environment is today as real for the child of the otherwise self-sufficient families as for the child of a deprived background. Children from either background need group experiences to augment the lags that are part of the small circle of today's family. Smallness of family groups, geographical as well as emotional isolation, environmental pressures may create climates that are not conducive to the healthy, comfortable development of young children.

I have attempted here to list some of the needs of preschoolers that are not fully met in their own home environment but which can be compensated for by appropriate group experiences.

SOCIALIZATION

Children, once they have left the toddler stage behind, have to have contemporary companionship for normal, healthy social growth. Social isolation may affect the child who lives in the city as much as the child who lives in the suburb or in a rural environment.

The young high-rise apartment dweller's access to contemporaries is not as easy as is often assumed. Companionship for him depends on the age of the neighbor's children, on parental relationships with neighbors, on the need for privacy on the part of the apartment residents, on available supervision that insures the child's safety as he goes visiting or invites a friend to his home.

In the suburb and the rural area the closest neighbor with young children may live blocks or miles away. A visit to a friend's or relative's house necessitates adult planning. Transportation may depend on availability of public facilities or may conflict with a sibling's football practice, the mother's PTA responsibilities, or the father's train schedule.

Suburban as well as city streets, where previous generations of children could congregate and casually encounter contemporaries, are now busy traffic arteries and no longer safe.

Playgrounds and parks are seldom within easy access of either group of children, and visits there again are dependent on adult schedules. The same holds true even for playgrounds built into high-rise developments. The preschooler whose family lives beyond the ground floor cannot be let out to play there by himself. Long-distance supervision does not provide the safety necessary for the very young.

ROLE ACCEPTANCE AND ROLE CHANGES

The young child's socialization is greatly influenced by the way in which he perceives himself. This process is affected by the way in which others see him and by their reaction to him. His role at home may become defined by his position in the family at a very young age. He may be an oldest or a middle child early in life. He may be and remain an only child or the youngest one. He may be perceived at home as a unique genius catered to by everyone and thus develop the idea that this is his due. Conversely, he may be considered a nuisance to be pushed aside and thus begin to think of himself as not worthy of concern and consideration.

The only child is likely to have had an undue amount of attention, both positive and negative, focused on him. He is, at home, never equal to those around him. He may find himself indulged in his inabilities, or measured against the greater abilities of others, pushed into unequal competition and criticized for his short comings.

The youngest in a very large sibling group is in a similar position, indulged and criticized alternately to his own confusion and frustration. He finds himself surrounded by too many bosses, since the older children find him fair game as a butt for their own frustrations and lack of power.

The pre-schooler who is the oldest of one or more siblings may find environmental expectations quite beyond his abilities and inclinations. He may perceive every other child as a very unwanted and unnecessary rival. He may consider others targets for his bullying or, conversely, much too early develop an attitude of resignation about having to give in.

The middle child feels himself quite surrounded with no special position for himself. He feels pushed from above by the older siblings who have always been there, and from below by the younger ones who nudged him out of his position as baby.

FAMILY CLIMATE

Family climate is not always conducive to a young child's happy development. Tension due to illness or emotional or economic problems may cause conflict between the adult's preoccupation and the young child's developmental and emotional needs. To illustrate this, let me describe a family I know. The adults are preoccupied with illness because of the serious health problems of several family members. Though the youngster in question was in perfect health he was not permitted the vigorous play he would have enjoyed. He was cautioned not to run so he would not fall and not to get overheated and become ill. Even moments of quiet reflection on his part were interrupted with some adult's anxious question regarding his well-being. A grandmother, an uncle or his own parents were sure to ask, "What is the matter? You have a headache? Are you not feeling well?" He learned much too early to be overly concerned with his health and to wriggle out of unwanted requests with a stomachache, a headache, or palpitations. He could not enjoy the gift of health and the pleasure of vigor and activity.

Overconcern for a child can have a stifling effect, but so has lack of interest or appreciation for a youngster's special gifts. This, too, can stunt growth and the development of these gifts.

CONFLICT BETWEEN CHILDREN'S AND ADULTS' NEEDS

Children need care, supervision, and developmental guidance regardless of adult preoccupations, inclinations, and schedules. Adults' and children's needs cannot always be comfortably met in the home. Demands on time by an invalid may cause disorganization in the family. Parental life style may serve the adults well but create confusion and cause lack of necessary structure for the child. The working mother's absences create problems both for the mother and the child, whether the mother works because of necessity or because of choice.

COMPENSATORY EXPERIENCES

Good pre-school programs can compensate for those social, emotional, and developmental experiences the home cannot provide for the young child. Trained teachers who are unhurried, who do not have to cook dinner, answer the phone, or run out to shop, can focus on the children and their needs. They can gear individual and group activities to the tempo and requirements of their young charges. They can provide a physical environment appropriate to the needs of young children and aid them in the development of social awareness and social skills.

Heterogenous groups assure wider experience for the child. Social contacts offer opportunity for the child to experiment with various social roles. He will find suitable models among the other children. Older, capable ones will help him set goals for himself. Younger, less capable ones may need his help and thus teach him concern for others and let him enjoy the experience of helping and leading. The neighborhood "bully" will have to accept group pressure toward toning down his assertiveness, and the shy, retiring child will have the opportunity to learn to defend his rights. Contact with different adults will help the child widen his horizons and develop self-confidence and comfort in the new situations.

He will learn new concepts of behavior: postponing immediate gratification of an impulse because there are others to be considered; waiting one's turn; verbalizing one's wishes instead of physically acting upon them (e.g., to reclaim a toy by asking for it back rather than snatching it); accepting school routines; and learning that in a group, if the teacher says, "All of you please come and sit down," he is one of "all of you." He will increase his attention span as he participates in a group activity, listens to music, or finishes what he has started. He will learn to understand simple game structure, such as: staying hidden when playing hide and seek and not telling where someone else is hiding (both things are difficult for a young child). He will learn simple concepts, such as what is acceptable behavior or what is polite, or the days of the week and their sequence. He will increase his self-help skills in an environment scaled to his size and ability. And, most of all, he will have fun with other children and find stimulation from doing things in a group.

PRE-SCHOOL PROGRAMS AND THEIR SETTING

Adequate group care for young children received a decisive shot in the arm in the early 1940s under the leadership of Leona Baumgartner and Cornelia Goldsmith. They established, within the framework of New York City's Department of Health, the first official Day Care Unit. For the first time there existed an agency charged with developing legally enforceable standards for the group care of children under six, regardless of whether they were enrolled in private or public programs. The multidisciplinary staff of the Unit came from the fields of early childhood education, public health, social services, and psychology. The most striking innovation, and the most important one, was that standards were established and enforced, not only regarding airspace, toilet facilities, and fire safety of a school. There were minimum standards regarding adequate staff and programs to meet the emotional and the educational needs of the young pupils in these agencies. The Unit offered consultation to those schools, day-foster homes, etc., that needed help in meeting standards for the care of the children they served.

Similar agencies sprang up across the country under public as well as under private initiative. Today many of these activities have been reduced because of lack of money and interest, not because of reduction in need.

Today, more than ever, we need sound direction and expert consultation with those who have experience in the area of early child development. We need level-headed people, professional and otherwise, to stem the flood of developing fads and the dangerous inroads made by big business, which has discovered pre-school education as a highly remunerative, still-untapped venture.

Undoubtedly the needs of programs for young children have changed with changing times. The basic early needs of the pre-schooler, his human needs for love, nurture, and time to develop, have not.

The quality of any school and the quality of its program depend on the quality of the staff and the leadership offered to the staff. Parent influence has become an important factor in the development of good programing, but it is important that the parent is motivated by real interest in the child's healthy development rather than in the creation of some hybrid educational showpiece. This will be further discussed later on.

There are many small schools that serve the children and their parents well by quietly pursuing appropriate goals and meeting basic needs. There is, however, a growing group lured by the promise of quick and flashy results of "teaching programs" that disregard the immaturity of their subjects and the highly specific emotional and social needs of the very young human being. Unfortunately, since the human child develops slowly, the effect of such "short-order cook" procedures in education will not become apparent until the damage is irrevocably done, and there can only be regret for having had a child exposed to pressures that he could not manage and that he did not know how to ward off.

It is worthwhile to look at a small sampling of such ventures advertised in the media, both the professional and lay publications. What recommends them is that they bear the label of being modern and venturesome. Many cater primarily to the vanity of the parent.

There are nursery schools that select their pupils on the basis of the child's future "college potential." How this potential can be determined in the three- or four-year-old is highly questionable. The child at that age is still even neurologically a very unfinished product, a long way from college entrance. Who knows in which direction he will develop? Considerable damage can be done to the children who are thus rejected from school entry as well as to those who are admitted. The child who is accepted may easily have to carry the onus of being a "genius" and "making it" from the ripe old age of three. He may tire of this responsibility and of the push and expectations connected with it by the time he is seven or eight and let some nice abilities go to waste. I have heard a bright four-year-old say provocatively to a teacher: "You've never seen anybody like me, have you?" Have those around him instilled in him the idea that he is outside the human pale already? If he sees himself at that age already as so different, how is he going to accept that he too has limits and needs adult guidance? The immature ego of a three- or four-year-old simply is not developed enough to weigh abilities and put them into perspective.

I have heard older children complain that there is no fun in being capable. It just means you are pushed from one subject to the next. You are never allowed to enjoy your brightness, to leisurely explore what interests you. You have to go on and constantly prove that you are worth bothering with.

The child who has been rejected by such a toddler's prep school may also be seriously affected. If parents are told by the "experts" that their child is poorly endowed and cannot make it in nursery school, they may feel that they have a potential drop-out on their hands. According to their own temperaments they may give up on him or they may begin to pressure him to achieve. Achieve what? They may begin coaching him in "studying" the "tests" necessary for the nursery school entrance exam. ("Don't play with your dolls or cars now. Learn to draw a circle, color within the lines. Here is another educational toy to make you bright.") It takes a fairly stable family to shrug off such an experience without being soured on the whole idea of nursery school and perhaps education.

Nursery school franchises have become big business. For example, *The Hour*, a local Norwalk paper, reports on a $10 billion industry in pre-school education—not in an "Education" column but fittingly under the heading of "Business Today." This outfit proudly proclaims that they will accept any child as soon as he is toilet trained, even as early as one year old. The children are taught to operate computers and closed-circuit TV. This, the franchisers say, "frees mothers to spend their time more profitably." One company reported on in *Newsweek* (November 20, 1972) develops "Montessori" schools on a "short-order" plan, guaranteeing a thirty percent profit. With such moneys and profits involved the need to show quick, dramatic success becomes infinitely more important than the emotional well-being of little children and their long-term need for even, well-rounded development.

A recent newscast showed a nursery school equipped to the tune of thousands of dollars with the very latest in the mechanization of young children. One of the sequences showed a three-year-old glued to a small computer. The computer intoned in an even, mechanical, never varying voice: "Find the small 'B.'" (The child pressed a button.) The voice again: "The small 'B' is in the cup. Find another small 'B.'" (Button pressed.) "The small 'B' is in the cup. Find another small 'B.'" Though the news item was comparatively brief, focusing on various activities in the nursery school, this one excerpt continued for a good minute or more. How long did it continue for the child?

"Find the small 'B.' The small 'B' is in the cup. Find another small 'B.'" Over and over and over. Hitchcock could have invented this scene as part of a child's nightmare. "What will he do with the small 'B'? What will the small 'B' do in the cup? Is it imprisoned there or will it come out?"

Why does the three-year-old have to find the small "B"? What has he learned if he can do this? Why does he have to sit at a computer like a keypunch operator at that age?

A teacher was standing nearby. There was no contact between teacher and child. She was neither talking to him, encouraging him, or freeing him from the clutches of the machinery that had gotten hold of him. The youngster's expression was intent and troubled. He showed none of the pleasure of achievement one would ordinarily look for in a child engaged in an absorbing activity. He was abandoned to a mechanical voice, the keys he pressed and the small "B." The adults were apparently fascinated and amused. When the newscaster appeared on the screen again at the end of the filmstrip he smiled. His expression said clearly. "How darling! The tiny tot working on a computer. And so intent on his task!"

Has anyone followed this child home to find out how he reacts outside of the school when the pressure is lifted? Does he show tensions? Has anyone talked to the parents to find out? The little circus animal has performed and his future fate is of little concern to us.

With so much money invested, of course the school would have to defend the program. Is this a first that will give the school an edge over competition? If this type of equipment becomes standard, will nursery schools too become education factories that have to serve large groups because it will not pay to use such expensive equipment for the small groups that are considered appropriate environments for young children? Simple, small programs will be quickly priced out of existence by the franchises, and, as we have seen in higher education, the large mechanized programs set up will play havoc with children's needs for identity and protection. The young child is particularly at risk because his undeveloped ego will not have enough strength to be able to fight anonymity before he becomes a number in an assigned slot.

What are the danger signs of tension indicating that a child is under too much pressure? Children have their own ways of expressing tension. They cannot verbalize something that they do not yet understand themselves. It is for the adults to be sensitive to the child's nonverbal signals.

One of the nursery schools I know of recently admitted a little girl at the urging of the parents. The school personnel felt that at two-and-a-half she was still too young for a group experience, but the parents urged them to try her. They were sure that she was ready and needed to be among other children. Because she was so bright they felt that she would be able to keep up with the rest of the group in spite of the age difference. Since this was a rather relaxed school, the teachers agreed to try her. The little girl herself seemed delighted and eager to go to school. However, within a short time she became irritable, burst into tears for no apparent reason, and had temper outbursts during which she would lash out at children and adults. The parents reported sleep disturbances and nail biting. It became quickly apparent that, though brighter than some of her schoolmates, she was not ready to handle the group situation. The very situation itself created a competition which was beyond her. When removed from the pressures to keep up with still undigestible stimuli and with social situations for which she lacked the necessary maturity, she quickly recovered her previous sparkling personality. Her family was helped to find other, less pressuring ways of enrichment, such as more frequent visits back and forth with one or two contemporaries; opportunities for imaginative play; outings with or without another child to the zoo or a museum; exposure to music; and so on. The family was also cautioned to be sensitive to her fatigue and satiation points and to allow for quiet periods for a highly sensitive, curious child.

The bright child even more than the duller one needs protection from himself. He requires the assistance of sensitive and interested adults who are aware of the less obvious signs of reactions to tiredness and boredom. No piece of machinery will be able to pick up tension and unhappiness in a child and react to it appropriately. If we rely too much on computer education, we ourselves may become inured to the understanding of human reactions in children.

Excesses are not yet the rule, but, particularly when large business enterprises become involved, they will have an insidious influence on the field of nursery education. The exponents of high-pressure training for the young are usually outspoken. Since such ventures carefully select their population and have very concrete goals, they can show much success. It is not difficult to tabulate increases in cognitive skills. And, if I.Q.s are based on cognitive performance, temporary increases in this area can also be tabulated. It is much more difficult to tabulate social or emotional growth, or to assist a less endowed child to blossom, which is not the same as teaching him to recite numbers and letters by rote.

If tasks are presented to the child in neat packages with clear-cut simple solutions, he will learn to deliver the expected answers. If he is taught by machinery that prevents error, he will not learn to try to figure out the steps leading to a solution. He will not struggle to understand a task and develop problem-solving techniques. He will assume that each problem has a single answer. He will have learned much too early how to pass tests, rather than how to acquire knowledge and find unexpected connections between problems and enjoy exploration of such connections.

The defenders of mechanical, drill training of the young do find support in the media because their ideas are innovative in a dramatic way and therefore make news. The more thoughtful defenders of the rights of young children do not often turn to the more popular outlets for ideas. They are wary of dramatic results and do not promise quick success or large profits. Their descriptions of how children investigate and accumulate information appears primarily in the professional literature and is unfortunately usually couched in terminology not suitable to newspaper or magazine articles. The same is true for warnings sounded about cramming children with mental food that they cannot yet digest.

To offer two brief examples:

Alfred A. Lucco in a thoughtful paper, *Cognitive De-velopment after Five* (American Journal of Orthopsychia-try, October 1972), discusses the disruption of the developmental organization in a young child who is battered with stimuli which he is not yet able to assimilate or ward off. I had a mental picture that is certainly an over-simplification and does not do justice to the author. However, I could not help visualizing a small corner grocery suddenly swamped by a large shipment of foreign delicacies. The grocer would not know how to merchandize the goods. He would have no space to store them in a way that would make them available on request. He could not bring order or system into the confusion of goods lying around. The disorder in a young child's mind created by a shipment of sophisticated concepts for which he lacks understanding and for which he cannot find a place in the immature nooks of his mind is quite as unmanageable and much more serious.

The other example comes from an article by Dr. David Hawkins (of Mountain View Center in Colorado), "Understanding the Understanding of Children." He offers a charming description of a three-year-old exploring the behavior of a pair of scales she found in the center's laboratory. Spontaneously she attempted to balance the scale by adding to the bowl which at the moment was higher and observing the effect. After a while she tried to find out what would happen if she added to the lower bowl, modifying her experiments in various ways. Nobody interfered with her absorbed activities. Nobody pointed out to her the principle of scales or offered the "correct" way of balancing. She remained fascinated with the activity for a long time. There was no shortness of attention considered typical for the three-year-old. It is hard to tell what the little girl "learned" while busy with the scales. (Who can ever really tell what a child learns? It certainly is not always what we think we teach.) Whatever she learned was real and satisfactory to her. She had experienced the deep enjoyment of absorbed activity. She had observed the effect of her actions and will certainly reach out for more and thus widen and enrich her circle of experiences.

To make a point of the absence of adult intercession may sound contradictory to the previous discussion of children's need for aduilt interest and involvement. Intrusion in a child's absorbed, constructive activity, however, is not involvement. The child mentioned above was happily engaged in a satisfactory activity. Adults would have been available had she needed them. To illustrate intrusive interaction of an adult, let me cite an incident I observed recently. In a nursery school where the "study plan" for the week was "teaching colors" I saw a youngster completely engrossed in playing with some colorful tiles. The teacher saw this as an opportunity to reenforce the week's lesson. She stated in a friendly way: "What a lovely pattern you are making." Then pointing to a tile she said, "Do you know what color this is?" The child looked up, smiled too, and said, "This is yellow." He promptly stopped the activity and put the tiles away. The spell was broken, the interest and absorption gone. The fascinating activity had become a "lesson." He had been working with arranging colors using equipment that had been provided by an interested adult. He was obviously aware of the colors he used. Pushing the point home was disruptive and not responsive to the child's mood and his own approach to experimentation and acquisition of knowledge.

Force-feeding cognitive facts, like all force-feeding, just spoils the appetite. It is not having the anticipated effect. Where academic force-feeding is employed to solve social ills, it does not work according to plan. The attempts to bring children from deprived, unstimulating backgrounds up to par with their more fortunate contemporaries with crash programs does not have the long-range effect expected. Follow-up studies indicate that the children are doing well only as long as adult interest and special attention continue. Crash programs apparently cannot make up for a steady diet of stimulation, interest, and care. Drill in cognitive rote learning, mechanical repetition and the fragmented presentation of *Sesame Street*-type programs cannot replace the constancy of a child's warm, personal stimulation by an interested and interesting environment. Recognition of shapes, even if the shapes are letters, is not the same as reading. Drill in correct phrasing of questions or answers and in naming objects does not necessarily develop language or stimulate the ability to hold a spontaneous conversation, which presupposes content and comfort with the other person. Experience with crash programs shows short-term effects which apparently disappear within the year.

Interested and interesting environments are not created

by mechanical means. The pre-schooler needs relaxed adults who can help him explore his environment and the people in it; loving adults who can provide for him situations where he has fun with others his own age, where he has the opportunity for imaginative play, and where he gets the aid he needs in his attempts to deal with social contacts.

If he graduates from the "cognitive crib" to *Sesame Street* to the mechanized nursery school, he will be "programed" for all kinds of knowledge that leave him empty, confused, and prone to early ulcers.

Many of the mechanical devices that have found their way into pre-schools were originally created to assist children with learning disabilities. The learning disabled youngster frequently has difficulties with concentration. He is easily distracted by what goes on around him. He may have difficulties remembering what he has been taught and needs considerable drill and repetition to stabilize his knowledge. Frequently he finds it easier to anchor knowledge when physically engaged by manipulating objects. He may be more successful and responsive to a mechanical device that he can manipulate, that can endlessly repeat and tell him whether his answer is right or wrong without losing patience or ridiculing him. It is to facilitate learning for these children that machines and isolation booths called "carrels" have been devised. The child who is in need of such special aides to learn can be helped to understand that isolation in the "carrel" is not punishment but will assist him to keep his mind on the task.

Such devices have now sifted down to the nursery

school where they have no justification. The pre-schooler needs to have opportunity to fit himself into a world of people and experience real responses from a living environment. He does not yet need isolation to concentrate on rote tasks. Exposure to mechanical drill in rote knowledge will only lead to much too early stratification of knowledge and fragmentation of thinking and learning. Mechanical approaches dull a child's natural gifts and curiosity. They are likely to give learning a nightmare quality at this early age.

During a recent visit in a school that grouped four- and five-year-olds together, I observed a four-year-old who had become involved in an activity with older children. Not understanding the activity he started interfering and disrupting. The teacher gently deposited him in a "carrel" with a reading machine. She briefly showed him how to operate the simple mechanism and put the earphones on him. Since she left him right away she did not notice the child's reaction to the situation in which he found himself. He looked like a small puppy indeed caught in a corral, not a carrel. He knew he had misbehaved and to him the isolation meant punishment, whatever the teacher's intention had been. He was abandoned to a machine that to him had no meaning at all. He was supposed to put a card on which a word was printed in a slot, and, as the machine moved the card slowly along a groove, a voice in the earphone intoned the printed word. Not only did the youngster have trouble inserting the card, he had obviously no concept of the relationship between the card and the voice in the earphone. It is quite likely that the teacher had demonstrated the machine before. But it was also obvious that the child was completely unready for the task. He did not dare leave the cubicle but kept looking around for someone to rescue him from the machine, from the voice, and from the isolation.

There would have been many possible ways of dealing with a disruptive youngster. The simplest way would have been to engage him in an activity for which he was ready and that would have had meaning to him. However effective and well thought out a machine may be, its effectiveness still depends on the learner's readiness and willingness to be engaged. The younger the child, the more will his willingness to engage himself in any learning process depend on his personal relationship to the people who engage him and to verbal contact with them. I remember one youngster, somewhat older than the one discussed before. She also was deposited at a machine to get some practice in reading. She seemed blissfully engrossed in the operation until it was discovered that she had turned the sound off and simply enjoyed the manipulation of the mechanism.

There are many other mechanical devices that supposedly teach "readiness" and in effect drain from learning its excitement and the feeling of unique achievement that comes from exploration and discovery. One of these devices is the worksheet, however, first cousin to the workbook.

A worksheet is usually a single sheet with line drawings of objects or geometrical figures. The task for the child is to color the form or object, staying within the line. This supposedly is a readiness drill toward reading and writing. In reality it has a dampening effect on interest and enthusiasm for learning and is deadening to the young child's imaginative abilities.

In one nursery school I saw a group of four-year-olds color a sheet of object drawings, most of which were certainly quite foreign to these children. There was an old-fashioned pocket watch, a wolf, etc. Those who had finished the task were given small sheets of white paper and allowed to draw what they wanted. The object at this point was obviously to keep the children still and seated rather than offer a stimulating activity. They drew circles, squares, numbers, and letters. Not a single child seemed to have an original idea about what to draw or to feel free to express himself. The children apparently were all well aware that this was "busy work" and knew what would please or impress the adult. And yet there was a whole beautiful world around them which they could learn to see, enjoy, and try to reproduce. Reproductions of real things, however, might not be as correct as the circles and letters; they might not intrigue the adults nor draw the same praise that was elicited by the four-year-old's ability to write the letter "A" or "M" or numbers up to 5.

I have seen the same sterility of ideas, the same lack of imagination and spontaneity already apparent in bright, capable three-year-olds of the *Sesame Street* generation when busy in their own homes. They draw letters and numbers. They ask adults playing with them not to draw them a dog or a house or a child, but to draw the letter *"b"* or the number 4. Finished achievement has become much more important than creation and exploration at much too early an age. The child who can "write" and "read" does not risk criticism of his creations from the adult.

With so much of the child's time in the nursery school being taken up with the teaching of cognitive subjects, little time and opportunity are left for the acquisition of life-related skills.

In the previously mentioned nursery school that taught computer skills to three-year-olds, the teacher later handed out small juice-filled cups. The young engineers apparently did not have the "maturity" to do this themselves. I am aware of few places where the children are permitted to pour their own juice or milk. The milk is sipped from the carton; the juice cups are filled in the kitchen. Cups and cookies are handed around by the teacher. There is less mess and less waste. Wasted is in reality an opportunity for the children to learn to pour cautiously, to focus attention on a fascinating task, to learn something about the behavior of liquid and of the relationship of measurements of jug and cup. Lost is the opportunity for a young child to learn to serve cookies to others from a platter without dropping them, to make sure that each child in turn gets his share. And lost is the opportunity for practicing the care needed to handle a flimsy paper napkin and experiencing the feel of its texture. Such skills would have reality for a child. They would teach, in a pleasurable way, awareness of others. They would teach organization and sequencing, since it is important that no one is missed as one passes around cookies, cups, and napkins. Such sequencing may have more impact than learning that "B" comes after "A" and 2 after 1. They would also teach awareness of others as the child notes the impatience of one child and the pleasant "thank you" of another. It would teach the simple social graciousness that the host or hostess serves himself last and will still have his turn.

PHYSICAL ENVIRONMENT

The physical setting is of prime importance in a child's successful group experience. The late Lili Peller, who pioneered in pre-school education, did extensive work in the effect of the physical environment on young children. Let us focus here on a few major points.

The physical surroundings of the young child have to insure his physical comfort and safety and offer opportunity for physical development. But there is more than this to a young child's tangible environment. Rooms, space, nooks, and corners invite exploration and present the child with the puzzle and the discovery of spatial relationships, the mastery of space, and the discovery that things look different when viewed from above, like the top of steps, and from below, as seen while crawling through a tunnel. The child in the group needs not only space to move about and run; he needs small, closed-in areas where he can gather himself together when he begins to "fly apart" because there has been too much stimulation and there are too many others around. He needs a nook where he can peek out and just observe for a while, look at a book, form a small community of two or three for imaginative play, or have an adult all to himself for a short time. The nook or closed-off corner in which the child can seek seclusion when he needs it is very different from the previously described carrel where isolation is imposed by the adult and used as a learning device.

Pre-schools need to be equipped with "child-size furniture," which is not quite the same as small furniture. It means furniture related to the size of the children who will use it. Since they come in different sizes, so should tables and chairs, with enough leg and elbow room for comfort and good posture and for the fun of trying out heights.

Since the development of self-care skills are such an important part of early education, the facilities for the development of these skills need to be an integral part of the functional arrangement of the room. Toilet facilities, running water, paper cup containers and towel dispensers need to be within easy reach of the child and so located that the adult can easily assist the child in learning to care for himself within the group setting.

These arrangements of the physical environment are important to the nursery school child as part of his development to aid age-appropriate independence. For the child in a day-care program they become an absolute necessity. The day-care child spends long hours in a group setting. The differences between routines and management at home and in the center may differ quite sharply. The long day is more fatiguing, and meals and rest hours may be more anxiety producing than playtime. The day-care staff has to provide much more mothering and catering to physical needs.

The daily rhythm in the day-care center has to take

into account the young child's need for vigorous physical activity, for the development of his mind and imagination, for emotional gratification, and for quiet, restful times. The child has need for active social contacts as well as for times when he can draw back, observe passively, play by himself, or select the company of just one or two others. Sensitive adults in a day-care setting will try to offer each child some time during the week that is all his own. A time on an adult lap, a short story, a quiet or lively game with dolls, blocks, or on the swings provide necessary breaks in crowded days. For the child from an overpopulated home this may be the only opportunity to have an adult all to himself. For the youngster who is used to closeness to his mother, it will ease the separation.

PARENT CONTACT

Contact with the parents is an important part of any program involving young children. It should mean exactly what the term implies—contact with both parents. Schools and agencies too often consider a child's mother the representative of the parents. The father, it seems, is frequently only included if the mother is unavailable or if there are serious problems. This pushes the father onto the fringe of relationships and makes him into the "disciplinarian," rather than an integral part of the family. The justification for this is that the father is too busy to concern himself with the rearing of his young children. Experience will show that most fathers have a lively interest in their young children and want to participate in their growing up. They simply bow to the tradition that rearing of the young is a woman's job.

Pre-school is the child's first independent venture. For the first time in his life he has an experience not shared by his family. It is also a first for many a young family. There is always some anxiety involved in such a first separation. While it is a step in growing up, such a separation should not interfere with basic family cohesion. Family participation in the school's program can strengthen both school and home goals for the child, assist the child in his adjustment to a new situation, and help him bridge the gap between the two experiences. While school, even if it is pre-school, should not be just an extension of the home, parents need to share in programing for a child's educational experiences. The parent should not be asked to simply hand over the child to the experts like a garment that needs cleaning or storage for a while.

PTA groups and regular individual conferences, plus an occasional visit of the teacher to a child's home, will help.

Parent participation in the school's program and cooperation with the school become particularly important in day-care settings. The child's more extensive separation from his home and the long hours spent at the center mean greater impact on child and family. There are also always certain problems that have led to the child's presence at the center. A working mother, physical illness, or emotional instability are likely reasons for the child's placement. Other problems may be inherent in the placement itself. Child and parents may overreact to being apart; the program or the length of the day may not be suitable for a particular child. Such problems need recognition. They have to be worked through and solutions have to be found. Social services should be part of any well-planned day-care program. A trained social worker can carry the main responsibility for parent contact and assist the parents with the handling of their problems. In order to leave the teacher free to relate to the children, the social worker can function as liaison between family and school. Because of her training and orientation, she can augment the center's services by focusing on the whole family. The child at the center is an integral part of his family and should not be viewed in isolation. Understanding the child's needs and demands can be facilitated by understanding the family's needs and background and the parents' expectations of the child. Adequate programing that serves the child and satisfies his parents can be facilitated by such an understanding. If additional services are needed, the social worker can spot the needs and facilitate appropriate referrals to a community agency. Any pre-school offers a unique access to families in need of services.

To illustrate this: In a local day-care center the teacher drew the social worker's attention to Amy S., a four-year-old who to them seemed inadequately cared for. She seemed often sleepy, carelessly dressed, and hesitant to return home when called for by her mother or a neighbor. The social worker had some difficulty contacting the mother. When she finally saw her, she found her troubled and careworn. Mrs. S. was quite aware of and unhappy about the lack of care she extended to Amy. All her time and effort went to a badly handicapped older child who needed endless attention and whose crying kept the whole family awake many a night. A referral to a special agency was arranged. Better medical care for the sick child and some homemaker service relieved the situation considerably. With this outside aid the mother was freed to respond to efforts to help her modify her own approach to the invalid and to Amy, to whom she could give more time and better care.

HEADSTART PROGRAMS

A word should be said here about Headstart. The original purpose of Headstart was to provide young children with some of the stimulation and structure which, for a variety of reasons, could not be provided in their own homes. Children from homes where adults were pressured and preoccupied with their own concerns were frequently found to lack structure and discipline as well as development of sufficient skills in verbal communication to enable children to adjust to the school by the time they reached regular school age. They lacked adult interest and stimulation and had little or no experience with play material. Headstart programs were first developed in order to aid disadvantaged five-year-olds with these experiences so that they might start school on a par with their luckier contemporaries. This meant helping them to accept a modicum of group structure, develop some ability to listen to an adult, to share, to become familiar with play material, to wait their turn in a group, to express their needs and wishes verbally rather than physically, to increase their attention span, and to help them lose their fear of strangers and of the school situation. These goals were not always clearly set and not always reached. Many groups were started with practically no equipment at all and were conducted by untrained personnel who were overwhelmed by the children's behavior and their own lack of knowledge of just how to introduce available equipment to the children. In some centers the single goal was to "establish discipline," whatever that meant, and however this could be accomplished without adequte staff, setting and equipment.

There were other centers that quickly became part of the school system with formal education pushed in the belief that intensive drill in speech, reading readiness, and number work would be a real headstart for these children. Since they were considered backward they were at some places programed with high school–type schedules. And, for these children who already were deprived of the joyful experience of play that would have provided the underpinning for their development of imagination, interest, and happy awareness of others, school life became very early a grim, task-oriented setting that turned them off, not on.

In such a setting adult involvement is easily confused with adult intrusion, which, instead of assisting the child, interferes with his activities and may cut short the child's absorption with what he is doing, with his pleasure in an activity, and with the learning potential which is inherent in an activity.

Because of the divergence of programs and approaches, it is hard to say what the advantages or disadvantages of one or the other Headstart plans are. Some of the programs that were started with great aplomb were dropped for various reasons; others melted into regular school programs being extended down to include much younger children or a variety of organically handicapped children. Some have charted a course of complicated, often short-lived research. There is much pro and con about some of these programs that may be related more to the fitfulness of operation than to the idea behind it. Maybe if a middle ground could be found and adjusted to the needs of the particular population to be served there would be a useful program rather than a lever toward push and pressure on young children to learn something for which they are not ready.

THE DAY CAMP

Overnight camping, as a rule, is not offered to children under six, and for good reasons. The separation, the change of pace and routines for comparatively short periods of time are too demanding on young children and offer not enough returns. The pre-schooler cannot understand and master the temporary nature of the separation, the overstimulation that goes with living and even sleeping in large groups.

I know of one interesting plan in which the children

attending certain day-care centers were moved with the entire group outside the city to an overnight camp for periods of two or three weeks. There were daily evening visiting hours for the parents, most of whom worked. This kept the separation for these youngsters to a minimum, provided them with outdoor living and activities. There was enough carryover from the fact that they were with their own teachers and schoolmates. In spite of this, a good day program would have been more desirable. As observed, the meal time in a large dining hall and bedtime in large dormitories were quite beyond most of the children and created discipline problems that had to be handled with more firmness than was good for these young children.

Without getting into any extensive discussion regarding good camping here, one must consider the fact that many camps, whether overnight or day camps, are overstructured and do not serve the main purpose of camping —namely, to get children to feel part of their natural surroundings and become involved with the plant and animal life around them. They are too often too carefully protected from such natural encounters as grass, clean country soil, and small animals. There is considerable anxiety about scheduling every minute of the camper's day to keep him out of trouble. There is no time left for the child to sit under a tree and watch bugs moving around, listen to birds singing, or simply enjoy a *dolce far niente.* In the process the child is likely to miss a lot that the out-of-doors would have to offer. Where day camping is made available to young children it is frequently just a somewhat adjusted nursery school program. Its main purpose may be the child's safe-keeping (what Fritz Redl calls "cold storage") and the relief of the parents, rather than the offering of something unique and exciting to city children who think that eggs grow on trees and milk comes from cartons and who have never seen a garter snake or a snail in the woods.

V.
THREE R'S IN THE FAMILY

TO RELATE, TO RESPOND, TO BE REASONABLE

In the face of ever further encroaching mechanization and commercialization on our lives, we have to protect human values for children with all the fervor at our disposal. The idea that human values may get lost to a generation of the very young, to be replaced by machines that offer concrete knowledge in their place, raises a specter of science-fiction dimensions. The machine seems to be able to replace aspects of human relationships without concern for the subtle values of the human relationship. One can now dial a prayer, have a medical diagnosis made by computer, and give the patient the computer-determined treatment. There are even some psychiatrists now who propose the use of tape recorders by both patient and therapist to replace the intense human relationship and human understanding that should form the basis of the therapeutic effect of psychiatric treatment. The tendency seems to be to more and more dispense with real live human relationships. That such possibilities now lie within our reach, and can be scientifically worked out and presented as values, arouses serious concern in those who care deeply for people in general, and for young children in particular.

Young children are impressive. The matrix of their experience is still quite blank. Educators point out that it is the earliest learning that makes the deepest, most lasting impression on children's minds and, one should add, on their psyches as well. They will invariably fall back on early learned and experienced values when they are in difficulty and need a point of orientation. To permit machines to imprint this matrix with clichés and stereotypes is an unconscionable waste of precious humanity. To present children too early with mechanistic, static absolutes may easily preclude their development of awareness of the subtle values which are not absolute and static, which are not measurable, but which present an infinitely important framework of orientation of deep emotions which have to be experienced rather than mechanically described.

DEVELOPING RELATIONSHIPS

Success with human relationships is an irreplaceable ingredient for successful human development. Its importance within the primary family (that is, parents and siblings) increases with the changing pattern of our lives. Today's young family is almost completely dependent upon its own small radius of parents and children. It lacks the underpinning of support from an older, more experienced generation. The often very young parents have to carry the full load of responsibility for those dependent on them. Relatives are frequently too far away geographically and too little involved emotionally to be able to provide stability at times of upheaval and assistance in time of need—from hand-holding, to baby-sitting, to care during a major crisis.

Relationship is a basic prerequisite of successful child-rearing. It is within the framework of comfortable relationships that helpful structure and discipline can be developed for children. These relationships form the keystone which will enable children to grow up satisfactorily; to orient themselves in life; to cope with adversities; to develop their potential for enjoyment, for learning, and for enriching their own lives and those of others.

To short-change children in their experiences with people to whom they can comfortably relate is to deprive them of the very soil in which they can thrive. To provide them with technical means of orientation and guidance may make them independent of adults to an undesirable degree, since it will remove them much too early from the influence of those people who have to help them develop and adjust. To push for too early independence will mean a serious loss of much richness in their lives. They will miss out on human warmth and care; on the happiness of being important to someone; on guidelines and on the possibility of developing judgment. Young children need a measure of dependence. If the adults who are responsible for them and for their early orientation to humanity abdicate their responsibility, the child may be left to develop his standards from the ever-present machinery and accept automated clichés of behavior and reactions, which, since they fit everything, really fit nothing.

It is too often now the puppet in the shadow box which tells a child what to do or how to feel. Whether it is Big Bird or Batman who is trying to orient the child regarding his behavior and feelings, we cannot permit shadows to replace real people in children's lives. We cannot permit machines to present simplistic, synthetic solutions and promote coarsening and sterilization of our lives. The current generation of adults still knows that there are other ways to live than by the standards of the Cookie Monster. (For those who do not watch *Sesame Street*, the Cookie Monster is one of the puppets in the famous series.) He certainly makes a poor model for identification for the young. We have to make sure that the upcoming generation of children will also know about the human values in life.

It is the media in general which have taken on the task

of shaping our attitudes toward life. It is not only the "kiddie show" which tells children how to live and what to do. The ever-present advertising of our technologically advanced ways is reaching into living rooms and bedrooms, shaping our patterns of adaptations. We are warned of the terrible danger of daily living. Fear and anxiety seem to be the most effective means of selling products. "If you do not brush your teeth with Brand X, you will have more cavities." You cannot, and you must not, stand pain for a minute if it is your pain. Pop a tablet quickly." "You will be old and unattractive right now (at age six? sixteen? when?) if you do not use Product Z." The very coffee we drink is advertised as if it were a deeply emotional experience on which a successful marriage depends. Where will children turn to develop some proportion and have their anxieties assuaged?

Young people are criticized for the coarsening of their manners, for their infatuation with indecent movies and with crazy fashions. We need to remember that it is not the young teenager who makes those movies and designs the crazy fashions. And it is not the teen who writes the ads which promote the trend toward "openness" by discussing hemorrhoids during the breakfast hour, nor do they write the script for the actor who talks about his bad perspiration problems while the family sits down to dinner.

It is not the young generation which has thought up the exploitation of the cute tyke who charmingly tells the doting grandmother that her breath smells. The real-life child may find it hard to understand, then, why the real-life grandmother's shock is not related to the realization that she is a smelly old woman who needs to mend her ways, but to the child's bad manners and lack of sensitivity.

To counteract the corrosion of the human fabric of life, we need to reestablish for children and for ourselves a framework of human relationships and human concern so that we can comfortably function and live together as people, not as programed machinery.

In a highly mechanized world where people are "programed" for function and reaction, emotions seem to be pushed into the background, and human relationships do not seem to matter much. If machines and goods can provide automatically for everyone's satisfaction, there is little need to be concerned about the feelings of others. The car, the telephone, the home laundry, all meant to facilitate and enrich our lives, also have a tendency to impoverish them. Sitting in the car, one is isolated from one's surroundings physically and emotionally. Things and people move by quickly as on a screen and can be spotted only superficially in passing. One may see the neighbor next door driving to the market without observing a troubled look on her face that would have made one stop and inquire during a personal encounter. A casual telephone inquiry of "How are you?" is merely a social form, not meant to be taken literally. In a personal encounter the answer "I am fine" will be modified for the observer by "body English" that translates the "I am fine" into real feeling and will spark a deeper, more real interest and empathy with the other person. The "fine" may may mean "I am troubled about something" or "I have had very good news today," and it can be responded to appropriately.

Modern, mechanistic approaches create a climate where there seems to be little need for children to develop awareness and consideration for mother and her workload. However dirty you get your clothing, there is the miracle cleaner and the double-load washer. The ad mother never gets annoyed with her children who rub dirt into newly washed shirts two minutes after they are out of the laundry. It is just popped back in. The "Bold One" is celebrated in song as he blissfully runs off to get himself as dirty as he can again.

On the other hand, the dissatisfaction of the young parents with their roles as housewife or breadwinner is incessantly reenforced by ads for shortcuts and products. The parents are exhorted to put the young baby in the baby swing where he can amuse himself without their involvement; to use a bottle tender to feed him so they don't need time to hold or burp him. They are told that their children will criticize them if the kitchen floor yellows and be upset if their father still drives last year's car without air conditioning. They are told to serve an endless array of frozen and canned foods to avoid being the kind of drudges who prepare freshly made dinners.

Concern for others, awareness of them, and sensitivity toward them is not taught by the puppet, nor can it be acquired satisfactorily from a course on human relations, parent effectiveness, or sensitivity training. Satisfaction with the small things in life cannot gain a foothold when the reasons for dissatisfaction are constantly emphasized or are feebly counteracted by the sentimentalized pseudo-ethics of the daytime serial. The complete invasion and the cumulative effect of the machinery that spouts homilies all day long and insinuates itself into all areas of our lives can easily be underrated. The impact on the child of the movie, TV, and radio generation, which has grown up with this synthetic concept of life, is all pervasive.

Concern for others and responsiveness to the needs of others cannot be taught by impersonal media. Such concerns develop naturally for the child who himself has experienced concern, whose needs are being met, and who, in his day-to-day living situation, is helped early toward awareness of others and of the feelings of those around him. In the close-knit family where children are enjoyed and are part of the family fabric, awareness of others becomes part of the consciousness of the young child early. In many small ways his own needs are mirrored in the needs of others around him. The playful "Let Daddy taste your lollipop" helps the very young baby experience joyful sharing and lets him see the parent as a person who, like him, enjoys a treat. The adult's response to his moods, to his laughter and his tears, forms a bridge between him and those close.

I remember the misery of a young man who stated that he was raised in an orphanage and therefore did not know how to be a father, having lacked the experience himself.

PHYSICAL ASPECTS OF RELATION-SHIPS

Closeness and relating have physical aspects that have become unduly suspect in our society. We are still carrying a Puritan heritage that suspects and damns sexuality in every touch of the hand. The fact that we have now elevated the four-letter word into high society and sexualize all experiences down to the very soda pop we drink and the toothpaste we use only underlines this fact. The longing for something that has been missed in the very early experiences of the young and growing child is not gratified by these automatic "band aids" in later years.

Babies in many strata of our society get less and less warm physical contact even if they are not confined to the Skinner Box,* which fortunately is much too expensive for the average household. But, in our equipment-happy times, there are other inexpensive devices that undercut the need for physical contact. The infant carrier certainly makes baby easy to transport, and he can be left safely strapped in almost anywhere. The automatic infant feeder saves time for the mother. But both deprive the baby of being held against a parent's warm, breathing body; they deprive him of the physical stimulation provided by the petting, holding, and moving in concert with another human being. These devices deprive the very young child of the gratifications that indeed may set a pattern for later warm and satisfactory relationships, and they do not supply the physical stimulation that is so important to his thriving, as Margaret Ribble has pointed out. They also deprive parents of a very enjoyable experience that is rightfully theirs.

I have heard a young father anxiously inquire

---

* The Skinner Box, named after its inventor, is a large plastic box where a baby may be kept without clothes or diapers. His moods can be controlled by lowering or raising the temperature in the box. No need to handle, clean, or comfort the child.

Three R's in the Family

whether there was something wrong with his four-year-old son, who loved to sit on his lap and wanted to be petted and kissed. Was he already afraid that his child was a "sex deviate" at that tender age? Why should parents and children be deprived so early of perfectly human, normal gratifications that have to be made up later by artificial means, by therapy, by group therapy experiences, and by much too early juvenile petting and necking. These are substitutes that never really satisfy primary needs.

These attitudes, in part, have to do with our anxieties regarding over stimulation of young children, which seems strange enough in view of the overstimulation they receive through the media and some modern play things. The other part, however, has to do with the need to force quick maturation and independence. Holding hands, hugging, and other expressions of tenderness are considered baby stuff to be outgrown quickly. Our negative attitude toward tenderness is certainly mirrored in our speech. We have few expressions for endearment and love, and it is interesting to compare the dearth of expressions for the tender aspects of life with the innumerable expressions at the command of the sportscaster, who can give a fifteen-minute report without once repeating a word for the way another team has been trounced, beaten, flattened, etc.

INDEPENDENCE

Dependency needs are viewed with uneasiness by a society that is becoming increasingly uninvolved and inclined to deny the importance of interdependence as part of human relations. A certain amount of dependence is necessary and pleasurable. For young children dependency is an invaluable ingredient for growing up, for feeling loved, and for being able to develop interrelationships and concern for others.

Independence, prematurely pushed, leaves the child floundering. It makes him much too early independent of adult influence. It deprives him of environmental assistance in achieving adaptations that are important if he is to find and give satisfaction. Premature independence forced onto young children by the adults responsible for them comes dangerously close to abandonment, regardless of the underlying motives. The child who is pressured into making his own decisions and fending for himself before he is ready is not becoming a comfortably independent youngster. He will be inclined to cling and force adult attention in areas that he could perfectly well manage himself. And he may select for self-determination those areas that remove him from adult influence and are likely to create discomfort for him as well as for those around him. We all know the child who, at an early age, will insist on his own social arrangements regardless of family plans but becomes panic stricken when he is to go to bed by himself; or will refuse to stay with Grandmother or Aunt if Mother wants to leave him there. What was considered development of independence may become an instrument of control of the environment to the detriment of all. I know of at least one child who, at the age of four, insisted that her mother feed her. If mother did not comply with her demands, she would use the telephone in her own bedroom to complain to Grandmother, who would then interfere on her behalf. She was not a child of affluent parents, only of very misguided ones who were struggling against their own immaturity.

The child who is forced into independence before he is ready soon becomes very difficult to live with. The four-year-old who is permitted to determine his own bedtime and resists any kind of bedtime routine, or the six-year-old who is considered mature enough to select his own school luncheons, will neither get the amount of sleep he needs nor the food he requires. The adult who has decided that the child is mature enough for such independence will become concerned over a child's nutrition and bothered by the youngster's manipulation of bedtime, and will be apt to resort to manipulative behavior on his own part. It has to be the adult's task to determine how much independence a child can handle at what stage in his life, and it is up to him to make a definite decision where this is indicated. This will make life easier not only for the adult but for the child even if he at first protests adult decisions.

RELATIONSHIPS—THE ADULT ROLE

Good human relationship depends on many small and subtle ingredients. These are part of human development, which is something that has to be experienced— lived through rather than be taught. Good relationships in a family are usually not very impressive for outsiders and do not make captivating TV scripts. If they have grown out of early mutual satisfaction, they are likely to be undramatic. Normal, healthy, happy development has no public appeal. It is difficult to dramatize on the screen and has no strong impact on the onlooker. Normal, even development spells, however, stability and emotional satisfaction for the individual involved, even if it cannot be viewed on the home screen.

Comfortable relationships within the family depend to a great degree on adult availability to the child, not only during major crises, but as a preventative of crises. The mother who feels that she need not be present when the youngster returns from school because he is trustworthy for an hour or two alone at home misses a subtle point. The child may indeed be trustworthy. Mother may justify her absence by pointing out how little attention the child pays to her after his return from school. However, an empty house has a very depressing effect on children. The feeling of loneliness or abandonment can become quite overwhelming. Though the child may be aware that the feeling is unrealistic, it may still be very real to him. This is doubly true if there is no compelling reason for Mother's absence, such as her need to work, to stay with an ill relative, etc. The return home after an absence, however brief, carries certain emotional overtones for a child that feed into his relationships. The child may indeed run out to play after a snack on his return from school. But he feels expected and enjoyed when mother is waiting. The outward expression on his return may belie these facts. They are nevertheless true.

If there has been a minor crisis during his time away, Mother will notice and respond then and there. She may provide opportunities for the youngster to talk about his troubles, or she may respect the child's reluctance to talk about it and file her observation away for a little later. If she has not seen him on his return, and there is no pattern of greeting and acting that can be observed, this closeness and sensitivity will not develop. The wise parent will never pressure a child about what happened when the youngster is obviously troubled and does not want to talk. But she will make sure that there is a quiet time which may lead to his opening up.

As important as Mother's awareness of the child's mood on his return is his budding sensitivity toward his parents' life apart from what directly affects him. He, too, may note on getting home if something has happened, and he will ask about it, then or later. Parents are often inclined to shield children too completely from upsetting incidents. Whatever happens in a family will eventually affect the children. If they are not permitted to share in all aspects of family life, there will occur a rift that can have deeply adverse effects. That does not mean that parents will pile all the grim details of an upsetting experience on the children. But a brief explanation that fits the child's age and maturity will tell him that he is indeed part of the family. It will make him understand adult preoccupations, and he will develop empathy with the feeling and mood of others. He will also see his parents as human beings with deep feelings and concerns that find expression in their behavior. He is then not the only one in the family upset by feelings of sadness or anger or disappointment. He can see that giving expression to these emotions is part of being a person, and that maintaining certain controls over one's feelings is part of growing up. These are important lessons to be learned by the growing child. And he has to learn them from those to whom he feels close.

Even as children learn more and more to manage for themselves as they get older, they cannot really dispense with adult presence. We need to remind ourselves of the steps a child takes toward independence and toward establishing his own code of behavior. The toddler has little control over his impulses. His saving grace, as Freud has pointed out, is that he is quite small and powerless. His rages can't really hurt, and his intentions are still fairly simple and overt. They can usually be anticipated, and he can be prevented from an act that could do serious damage. He can be stopped by the gentle physical intervention of an adult or, a bit later, by signals verbal or otherwise that he has learned to understand and is beginning to respect. Then comes the time when he will remember instructions because of the mere presence of the adult which offers support to his striving to please. Gradually the child internalizes the external structure and can to a fair degree remember what is acceptable and what is not. He will strive to meet standards, even if he is not always successful. Only much later is a youngster able to evaluate codes of behavior, modify and translate what he has learned to changing situations and to his own inclinations as well as to the code of his particular group.

There remain times throughout most of childhood and early adolescence when the adult's presence stabilizes children, even if there is no actual adult intervention. This, too, is part of relationships. The teacher in a classroom may not be actively involved with the students, but her presence has a calming and reassuring quality. A mere glance in the direction of incipient trouble may remind the children of standards that were agreed upon. It is just much easier for children to refrain from misbehaving than to stop themselves once started.

In the home, times of heightened activity, of pressure, or of low resistance against irritation particularly demand an adult's presence, a fact that is often overlooked by parents, especially when they are at their own low point. Usually, neglecting to meet subtle demands for adult involvement in a potential trouble situation at the right moment, leads to forced involvement later on. Such forced involvement is likely to be unsatisfactory to all concerned. The early morning as well as the late afternoon hours are such times of special stress. We might illustrate this with an actual situation which, though specific, has a quite general application.

The situation in point concerns a family of four children. The mother had turned to a local clinic for help with the children. She could not understand their endless bickering among themselves and their unmanageability. The most difficult thing for this mother was the constant fighting in the early morning. As it turned out, she could not face this phase of the day and preferred to stay in bed until the children were off to school. She admitted that she had never prepared breakfast for them and had relied on the oldest from the time he was little to put cereal and milk on the table. By the time he was six or seven, he would cook an occasional egg or fry a piece of bacon for the younger ones. This older child had never complained about having to feed everyone, and Mother presumed that he did not mind. She could not understand his acute dislike for his younger siblings, and the dislike of all of them for each other. She felt that they all, including the youngest (who was then four), were perfectly capable of caring for themselves and did not seem to need her. She was puzzled and angered by the complaints from the school about the children when they turned up without lunch, without coats on a cold day, or without their gymsuits. She knew they were able to remember what they needed, and often had prepared for their needs the day before. She had to travel endlessly to school to bring lunches or homework that was left on the kitchen table or to take a child home because he had arrived for classes too distraught to fit himself into the school routine.

The mother was finally prevailed upon to try to join the children in the morning to see whether this would make a difference. She was surprised at the almost immediate relaxation of the atmosphere, the children's improved ability to get along with each other, and their ability to remember what they needed for school. Her mere presence was supportive and calming regardless of whether she prepared breakfast or let the children take care of their own.

MANNERS

Manners are an important part of positive human relationships. Because manners are looked at askance these days, we forget how reassuring and supportive manners can be to a child who has aquired them early and naturally. They provide for him guidelines of behavior in strange situations where he would feel awkward and would not know what to do. Manners can supply for the child a measure of security and poise. If he is embarrassed by an awkward act, he can say, "I am sorry, I did not mean to do this"; and if he is embarrassed by unexpected praise he can say, "Thank you." Of course manners, like traditions, are a matter of form, but they can be provided with content. They can be taught as a way to express concern for others and an attempt to make others comfortable. Children who have never developed manners and are used to undisciplined or rude behavior often feel quite uncomfortable in strange situations. They know that their behavior is not acceptable and are uncertain about how others will react to them. They have no comfortable techniques of making others like them and prefer to not expose themselves to rebuke where they are unsure of their ground. Thus, they prefer to stay away from new encounters and thereby deprive themselves of enjoyable experiences.

VI•
STRUCTURE

Structure, authority, and discipline are quite suspect in today's America. These terms are likely to conjure up a specter of Hitler, of violated civil rights, of encroaching communism, of 1984. What structure? What discipline? For whom and to what end? How important are these concepts to the development of relationships?

Let us view some of the problems besetting the young family that sets out to develop reasonable structure and discipline for their offspring and let us look at the cultural setting that makes such attempts difficult.

THE NEW NOMADS

One of the conditions that disrupts the attempts of young families to set reasonable structure for their children and develop adequate discipline is the high mobility of today's families. This is particularly true for the younger age groups.

As stated earlier, today's nomadic society does not have the clan support that previous nomadic societies had. Then, it was only the inanimate environment that changed. The human surroundings remained stable. For today's nomads, the whole fabric around them changes and falls apart. Anna Freud observed during the Blitz in London that young children were quite oblivious to danger as long as they stayed with their mothers, or with people to whom they felt close. This seems to hold true to a certain extent for adults as well. Difficulties are less overwhelming within a familiar environment and with the support of ties to loved ones. Separation from those emotionally close is threatening. Moving to another location, and to still another one, means pulling up roots, discarding friends, and losing the support of those one knows. Friends, because they love one, accept peculiarities and put up with one's whims. Strangers are inclined to be critical and judgmental.

It is quite possible that some of the familiarity people look for in new surroundings is found and treasured in the sameness that is created in our far-flung environments, the sameness of the chain stores, the food markets, the shopping centers; and last, but not least, of TV shows and radio programs. These may be the only points of stability nomadic families can find on their peregrinations.

Frequent moves, not rare for young families, leave them isolated and vulnerable. Standards are likely to change with the ever-changing locale. The young family misses a framework of orientation regarding appropriate standards for themselves and for their children. They are likely to flounder and vacillate about setting standards and about following a clear line of establishing discipline for their offspring. Erikson points out that the very tolerance of which we are so justly proud in this country also deprives us all of a hard core of orientation and identification. Undercurrents against providing standards and discipline for the growing child are strong.

"Setting standards? How can we? The world is changing too fast. Today's standards will not serve my child when he is grown."

"Establishing discipline? He'll hate me if I don't permit what Amy, next door, is permitted." (And it may be a different Amy twice a year.)

"Setting home rules? I don't want to confine my child. He needs to be free, develop his own judgment, make his own choices and mistakes."

It sounds good and modern. But does it work?

"What's a mother to do?" says the commercial.

It may be easier to relinquish responsibility than to try and find one's way through the maze of changing environments and attitudes and fight the ever-ready, simple answers of the mechanical problem-solver in the TV room.

"You can't tell today's children what to do. They know more than we do. Let them find their own way."

We forget that children have always resisted following directions and accepting authority. To resist is for them a way to learn, to test, to sort out what works and what does not work. They learn what they can get away with, and what is worth the price they have to pay for infringements. Where adults were clear and honest in their demands and in accepting their own role as responsible adults, where authority was reasonable, children accepted it. And children accept it today in the majority of stable, reasonable families.

Do children really know so much more today about finding their way in a complicated world? They certainly have more information. They know at very early ages about ecology and about electronics. They can do the new math in grade school. They can use $64 words and often know what they mean. They can spot the weak link in adult behavior and know how to verbalize their criticism. But they do not really know more about those things that are acquired by living through a situation, by understanding the forces that influence decisions. They cannot know about the multiplicity of living conditions, and—not having had the experience—they cannot easily anticipate the reactions to and consequences of their own actions. They can make good choices and use good judgment in a limited way only when they know the range and the interrelated effect of certain choices. And they will find that it is hard to judge situations that cannot be seen in their full complexity.

GROUND RULES

Developing a sense of perspective and proportion takes time and guidance. The child who grows within an environment that provides reasonable, flexible structure that can be modified as the child matures, will find his way with a certain amount of ease. He may fight home rules and regulations, but feels secure in the knowledge that responsibility will not be his beyond his ability to manage, and that his parents and teachers will stop him from misbehaving before he really comes to grief.

Good structure is not an arbitrary edifice that serves the comfort of the adult or is geared entirely to the child's needs. It has to be logical and flexible to insure comfort for the whole family. In our child-oriented society, we may forget that the child is part of a family and of a community fabric. His rights can be protected only within this fabric that insures *Lebensraum* for all.

The "civil rights" of the very young are their rights for protection, not only from others but also from their own, still untrammeled impulses. Their rights are for dependence on others, until they are ready to try their own wings, make choices, and explore alternatives; until they have an inkling of what is involved in taking responsibility for their own actions, and take the consequences of misjudged activities. Their rights are to receive help in developing judgment and gaining the necessary experience.

Good structure gives a child a frame of reference before he has learned to judge the limits of acceptable behavior and becomes aware of the reactions his behavior draws from those around him.

Whether today's structure and standards will serve the citizen of tomorrow is hard to anticipate. But tomorrow's citizen is still today's child. If he is to find his way ten or twenty years from now, he will have to have guidelines that have long-range value. He needs a set of ethics by which to guide his life. Some will find this guidance in religion, others in humanitarian philosophies, still others in practical, workable, everyday maxims. All have to receive the first indication that there are basic ethics which must not be violated from those they love and from those with whom they share their early lives and experiences.

The basis for such a code of ethics is that living together is a question of give and take, not a question of just receiving. Even the young child can accept the give and take of relationships if requests are within his ability and a natural part of the family pattern. Reasonable expectations of his cooperation will enhance his own self-concept as a full-fledged member of his family. This may be as simple a request as not keeping the family waiting when it is mealtime, or the more complicated one of assuming a daily chore like setting the table, to the more demanding one of being patient with the baby when he grabs for a treasured toy.

The process of learning is slow. The child needs time and the deep honest involvement of adults who love him. This will enable him to forego the gratification of needs that to him seem paramount and overwhelming. Only with time and patience will he learn to internalize some of his environment's standards, and find not only that he can survive environmental restrictions on his demands, but that gaining self-control can be an exhilarating experience. A reasonable code of basic ethics can serve the child and the growing young person for a long time to come. It can be modified as times and expectations change, yet it can insure a way of living that is human and satisfactory.

Structure is a set of do's and don'ts that fit the individual family of which the child is a part; that does not too seriously conflict with the fabric of the surrounding community; and that expands as the child grows and becomes ready for wider pastures. Such standards will include something as important to the development of social mores as, "You must not willfully hurt someone else physically or emotionally," or, "You do not help yourself from Mrs. Burns' refrigerator when you play in Sally's house"; to such family expediences as, "This is bedtime now," or, "I do want you to behave at Grandma's."

This kind of simple structure makes children easier to live with and combats the phenomenon, observed with misgivings, that we are very concerned about our children but find them often difficult to like. The undisciplined child, who is overly aware of his own rights and has little awareness of the reactions he draws from others by his behavior, is just not very likable. Lack of personal discipline seriously disadvantages the child now and especially later when his youth and parental lack of responsibility will no longer be a factor in making allowance for unpleasant behavior.

While the underdisciplined child is difficult to accept and live with, the overdisciplined one is, in his own way, just as difficult. He is likely to be unspontaneous, and unimaginative, and one can never know when he will suddenly and seemingly unreasonably cut loose and behave in a very unpredictable manner.

If serviceable standards and structure are to assure family comfort and child-rearing goals, they have to be developed with the growing child in mind. They should never be used to serve as a vehicle for adults to work out their own hangups.

There are many interesting and exciting new approaches designed to help children grow and develop. There is a new awareness of the so-called "soft signs" of delay of neurological development or slight neurological problems that can interfere with a child's learning. There are new methods in assisting these children early in compensating for such difficulties. But new programs for child rearing and teaching have to be carefully evaluated as to their underlying, not always obvious, purpose and effect. They have to be thought through in their planning and in their execution to make certain that they serve the planned purpose.

A young parent or teacher may try to resolve his own problems with authority and self-discipline by over-structuring the children under his care ("If they are not provided with a program for every minute of the day, they will only get in trouble"); or by setting no structures ("If you just let children run completely free, they will find their own level"). The overstructured child may respond to the straightjacket approach in two possible ways; by rebelling and fighting structure all the way; or by succumbing and giving up all initiative and imagination. The child who is let loose to find his own level may indeed do so, but those around him may find this level impossible to live with if there is no attempt to channel juvenile strivings.

Some new programs are misdirected attempts to have young children fight the adult's battle for social recognition. In a recent, I think short-lived, attempt to teach children of deprived backgrounds to stand up for their rights, the target was four- to five-year-olds. They were practically terrorized by the adults into stating that they were afraid of nobody and would not obey anybody. The adult would call on a child in the group and yell at him, "Are you afraid of anybody?" The child was programed to yell back, "I am not afraid of anybody," and so on through the whole register. The children, their baby faces frozen in fear, would give the required answers with quaking voices. I tried to visualize what would happen to those children who tried to apply what they had learned according to their own lights and logic. One had to wonder what Mother would say if she asked her offspring to go wash his hands for dinner and he yelled back in the same terror-stricken voice, "I obey no one. I am not afraid of you." Mother might have her own, unexpected reaction to this. And what about the child who tested out the newly learned response when asked for order and attention by the very teacher who taught him disobedience?

As stated, I think the attempt was short lived. The teachers may have found their theory untenable and turned to other ventures. But the effect on the children who went through this program cannot be eradicated that easily. What will become of them? The responsibilities of those who establish new programs and want to try out new approaches to the rearing of children have to be taken very seriously. They cannot simply be dropped when the researcher finds himself at a dead end. The experimenter has to take responsibility for the consequences of his experiment and be ready to remedy difficulties that occur in the wake of experiements that do not develop according to plan. The child is always the loser in poorly thought-through research that has been prematurely applied. He cannot cope with confusion created for him by conflicting adult requests and goals. The effect of poorly designed experiments can be widespread. Novel, unusual approaches to tenacious problems easily find their way into print and onto the TV screen often long before they have been properly tested. They may be eagerly snatched up by those who look for quick, easy solutions and form the basis for new fads that can affect great numbers of children.

CONTRADICTIONS

It is not easy to set reasonable, acceptable standards for children and young people in our contradictory times. While Americans throw up their hands in disbelief at the discovery that European children drink coffee at an early age, the American child is raised on Cokes by the gallon.

While the "highbrow" is viewed with suspicion, a college education is presented to youngsters as the ultimate goal in their lives.

While we deplore the time pre-schoolers "waste," children are permitted to spend endless empty hours in front of the TV, or in the family car en route to some errand or other, or in a school bus during hours that should be the most productive part of their day.

While we talk of our abhorrence of violence, the quality of a movie or TV show is practically rated by the number of punches traded and the number killed, and the who-done-it is favorite literature.

While we tell children that winning is unimportant, it is the game and the team spirit that counts, woe befall the Little Leaguer who believes this. He may have played his last game, and his father will no longer talk to him.

The list is almost endless. And again—"What's a parent to do?" The social contradictions notwithstanding, parents can set standards for their own children if they are willing to help their children understand the reasons for the house rules and regulations within their own particular family. Stable families with strong emotional ties can establish a code of living and behaving that suits the parents' and the children's needs. The child who feels close to and supported by his family develops pride in his family's standards and can meet the occasional taunts from his contemporaries. He may indeed at times gripe about his "deprivations" and let his buddies know that his parents cannot be reasoned with, but he will quite likely stay within limits and basically like them.

VII•
THE TROUBLING QUESTION
OF DISCIPLINE

Once the adults have a clear picture of the standards that need to be established, are honest about them, and are willing to abide by them themselves, putting them into practice is a question of discipline. For some reason the very term creates uneasiness in our times. Parents often respond to the suggestion that they establish some discipline for a recalcitrant youngster with, "How can I punish him? I cannot hit him all the time."

Good discipline has nothing to do with a spanking. It does not mean punishment. Good discipline means the establishment of the kind of structure that reduces the need for both punishment and spanking, not because the child is cowed into submission and would not dare misbehave, but because, if good discipline has been established early, the youngster knows what is expected of him and can work out his adjustment. He has learned that life has its rewards if he does his share of cooperating. He knows how and where to lodge his protest if demands seem unreasonable to him. He knows that he will be listened to and that demands will be modified if his protests are justified. And—and this is very important—he will feel protected by adults who will tell him when he is overstepping the boundaries of acceptable behavior. While sensible parents will let a child experience the consequences of trespasses, they will stop unacceptable behavior before the child really comes to grief. This kind of discipline means security and safety for a child. He will know that people care for him enough to put up stop signs and invest time, concern, and effort to see that he abides by them.

It is important for children to take the consequences of their behavior. This will help them develop awareness of their own actions and judge the severity of infringements. And they will learn something about cause and effect in relation to their own behavior and other people's reactions to them.

Here is a good illustration of teaching a child the cause and effect of his own behavior and responsibility for it. It shows the subtle mixture of a physical situation and its emotional components, as well as its responsiveness to adequate handling.

Bobby, age ten, was a somewhat clumsy child inclined

to react with violent temper outbursts when he bumped into things. His mother was casual in her housekeeping. Since she knew that the child had trouble avoiding bumps, she would always blame herself when he hurt himself on a piece of furniture that was slightly out of place or even the doorjamb that had not ever been moved. From the time he was little she would humbly take his tantrums and spank the doorknob or the table leg that had gotten in his way. Mrs. M. eventually sought help with the management of Bobby, who was getting more and more out of hand. After the child went into a rage for the hundredth time over bumping into an old washing machine that had stood in the same basement corner for over a year, the mother was finally able to separate her own unrealistic guilt from the child's unreasonable reactions. She told him quietly that he knew where the washing machine was and could walk around it. The child looked at her in surprise. He had expected the usual scene with the gratification he obtained from yelling at his mother. He also, apparently for the first time, realized his responsibility to avoid getting hurt, and, just as important, he realized that he had control over his environment in a more constructive manner. When adult reactions to his "accidents" became consistent and reasonable he could respond to adult attempts to help him manage his physical as well as emotional behavior better. He did not suddenly become a well-coordinated child, but he learned to recognize his shortcomings and find ways to minimize them. His mother tried quietly to make sure that there would not be unexpected obstacles in his way, but she no longer took responsibility for his running headlong into things. With unrealistic emotional reactions out of the way, realistic mangement had become possible in all areas of his behavior.

The establishment of good discipline does take time. The setting up of rules and regulations that are meant entirely for the convenience of the adult will quickly be spotted as self-serving, even by very young children. Such rules simply challenge the child's imagination to find ways to circumvent them. Most children are past masters at manipulating adults and testing the adult's ability to see unpleasant situations through. They seem on the whole more capable of figuring out how a parent will react to a given situation than parents seem able to anticipate their children's behavior. Any parent will be able to cite innumerable instances of temper outbursts at a public place when the youngster is denied a request. The child is sure that he can force his parent's hand when the parent wants to avoid embarrassment. And though this may happen time after time, many parents will find themselves caught "unawares." All parents have had experience with their children starting forbidden activities quickly when Mother is on the phone. And they know how children will try to flaunt all house rules when there is company. Such incidents occur occasionally with all children with little harm done. Children do need to taste a little power sometimes and occasionally get the better of adults. The secure parent can laugh it off, gently warn the child, and stop such behavior before it gets out of hand. If a child's manipulative behavior becomes the rule, the parent should be able to anticipate it. The child should be forewarned about the consequences of unacceptable behavior wherever or whenever it occurs, and his acting out should be undercut before it really gets started. A shopping trip may have to be cut short if a child is using the occasion for a tantrum. This may be highly inconvenient for a busy mother, but it will save time and trouble in the long run. If Mother knows from experience that her offspring will start a prohibited activity as soon as she is otherwise engaged, she needs to make sure that he too is busy while she is. How this can work is illustrated in the following example.

Danny, age two-and-a-half, had taken to attacking unsuspecting callers as soon as Mother opened the door for them. This happened so fast that it always seemed to take the Mother unawares. The youngster, though seemingly engrossed in his play, would dash up from nowhere the moment she admitted the visitor. It was suggested that she keep in mind what the child was about to do and delay the opening of the door long enough to seek him out. She would then tell him quietly that he was not to go after the visitor. He was taken gently but firmly by the hand as Mother went to open the door, introduced him to the visitor, and asked him to shake hands. The shaking of hands served as a mild substitute for the physical impulse. When the little boy no longer had the satisfaction of the attack accomplished, he lost interest in creating incidents that for reasons of his own had been so satisfactory to him.

While a child needs to be warned regarding the consequences of unacceptable behavior, the effect of too frequent threats of punishment which are not carried out will wear off quickly. They will be turned into taunts by the child. ("Look how bad I am. What are you going to do about it?") Behind such a taunt is usually the child's hidden fear of his own inability to stop himself and the wish to be stopped by someone more powerful.

It is never a good idea to make a threat that cannot be carried through. To say to a three-year-old, "If you do not behave, I shall leave you home all by yourself," does not make sense. He cannot be left home alone, and is probably quite aware of it. He still may be terrified if he sees the parents walk away from the house without him, but he knows they have to come back and get him pretty soon. They will have on their hands a very unhappy, angry, frightened child who may indeed behave for the next few hours. There's no long-range benefit from such an incident. The child will quickly find the chink in the parental armor, and the temptation to find out what will happen next may be almost irresistible for him. Anger and terror do not make for good relationships, and without good relationships there is no real cooperation and obedience.

It is a very different matter to send a child out of the room where everybody else is gathered if he is troublesome. The less punitive the adults are about it, the more effective this is. I have often heard parents say, "Being sent to his room is no punishment: he has all his toys there and he just plays." In spite of appearances, the child who is removed from the group feels unhappy and outcast. The main purpose of removing a misbehaving child is the interruption of his behavior over which he apparently has lost control. Removal gives the child time to reestablish some self-control. If he is told at the time of his removal that he may return whenever he is ready to be a pleasant part of his family, he is learning an additional lesson. He is learning to judge his own behavior. He learns about responsibility for establishing his own controls and about how to reestablish himself in society after he has disgraced himself. A misbehaving child often gets in a corner from which he cannot extricate himself. He needs help with this. Help is given, not by lengthy explanations and interpretations he does not understand and may misuse, but by giving him the opportunity to calm down by himself and start fresh. It is better, on his return to the group, not to ask him whether he will be good now. This may just remind him of his previous behavior and trigger a repetition. He should feel fully accepted when he reenters.

If a child has seriously infringed on the rights of others, if he has endangered himself or others, he needs to understand clearly what he has done and that whatever happens to him is a consequence of his behavior and not a whim of the parents. This is not an easy task. The angry parent is inclined to point out to the child what he has done to him, the parent. He may assure the child that punishing him hurts the parent more than the child. No child will ever believe this. The parent may talk too little or too much in such a situation. Young children are often given explanations that are way beyond them. They may stop listening after the second sentence if they cannot follow the explanation. They may get the same explanation over and over for the same kind of infringement, and, though by now they know the words by heart, the meaning gets lost in frequent repetition.

Conversely, children may get no explanation at all, just the sentence pronounced. They will not benefit from a punishment whose basis they do not understand. To be admonished to be good means very little to most children. The youngster was probably told he was good when he ate his whole dinner at home and told he was bad when he emptied Grandma's cookie plate. To him, both situations are pretty much the same. It is best to be brief when talking to a child. One might say, "I will not have you go across the street by yourself. It is dangerous." If the child crosses anyhow, he can be brought into the house and told briefly once or twice, if necessary, why he has to stay in. One can assume that he knows after that. His pained question, "What have I done? Why do you take me in?" might be countered with, "I think you know, and I think you can tell *me* now." To paint for the child an extensive, gory picture of what might happen to him if he were hit by a car is superfluous. If he is brought in immediately, he will get the message. The length of time a child is grounded should be related to the severity of the situation and to the question of repetition. To ground a child too long may lose its effectiveness after the first day or so. The child may no longer remember what he was grounded for, the parents may have forgotten, and the whole issue will become senseless. To tell a child to stay in for a week, and then let him go out because the weather is nice, he is a nuisance indoors and no one remembers anyhow what he is staying in for, will just teach him to disregard threats. Limits for the child's behavior as well as for adult reactions to this have to be reasonable and in line with the occasion.

DIALOGUE MEANS TALKING WITH— NOT TO—THE CHILD

As soon as the child is old enough to hold a conversation, it is a good idea to ask him the reasons for his unacceptable behavior. Such questions must not be threatening. The child who faces a stern adult saying, "For heavens sake, tell me why you did this! I have told you a dozen times not to hit Linda," will probably shrug his shoulders. His best defense is to say, "I don't know." End of dialogue. The adult who can quietly ask, "What made you do this?" and then wait for the child to gather his thoughts and struggle for an answer is more likely to gain some understanding of what happened. This does not mean that the child's explanation is accepted as an adequate reason for his actions, but there can be a dialogue.

The child will lie? Maybe. In that case, the adult can let him know that the explanation does not sound right and he would like to have the real one. Listening to children and really hearing what they are saying is not always easy. It needs patience and the ability to hear the things that have not been said clearly. One can help a child explain his actions. They may not be clear to himself as he starts out explaining them. What sounds like a lie may be his casting around for an explanation that clicks. He himself does not really know yet. The right kind of questions can help him to come closer, step by step, to what actually was in the back of his mind. This does not mean that one "feeds him lines." But asking the child to reexplain some of his statements will let him know what does and what does not sound plausible, may help him understand his own actions better, and will help him to verbalize. The child who is learning to put his thoughts into words may be a little less tempted to put them into aggressive actions.

This should not mean that the youngster is grilled after every infraction of rules, but, if there is much repetition of unacceptable behavior, it helps to understand why the child is acting the way he does. The adult can be sympathetic with a child's hurt feelings without condoning the act. Discussing a child's behavior and accepting his explanation does not mean that he should go scot-free because he has so beautifully explained the reasons for his behavior. If he deserves punishment the best explanation should not deter this. But the discussion can give the adult a lead as to how to help the child to avoid repetition.

I know of a youngster who got irritated at a neighbor who had left his Christmas lights on the tree outside for months after the season was over. So he and a friend had a grand time putting out the lights by smashing the bulbs. His explanation was detailed and beautiful. He felt it was religiously unacceptable to have Christmas lights on in May. Since he had given his reasons and was so logical and righteous about it, he was not punished, though he was told that his behavior was not acceptable. The parents felt quite justified in their handling of the situation since the child had given such a good, plausible explanation. Such parental reaction will only serve to re-inforce unacceptable behavior in children, who may get the idea that if you have a good reason for misbehaving, your actions are acceptable—you're off the hook.

The child who understands basic rules and regulations can orient himself and try to adapt to the environment. If he finds rules too confining, he can learn to negotiate changes rather than break rules. Compromises are often possible and work better than a rigid rule that invites flaunting. Children can be surprisingly astute regarding the necessity for ground rules and can be cooperative if they have had a voice in deciding priorities and how to enforce them.

Lack of home discipline easily leads to bickering among siblings who encroach on each other's rights. A family council meeting can often clear the air in such situations, if parents are honest about their wish to meet realistic needs and requests and take their share of responsibility.

Parents have to help all of their children to find realistic ways of adjustment. I know of one situation where a little boy made life miserable for the large family of which he was a part. He was not only the youngest in the family but had been quite ill, so that the parents indulged him and did not permit the other children to retaliate when he became difficult. Thus he did not have the usual, normal checks on his behavior and learned to dominate the whole household, children and adults alike. The siblings took their irritation with the little one out on each other. There was constant fighting between them. When the parents finally sat down with the whole group of children to discuss their behavior, they were startled at the pent-up irritation of the older children with their little brother. They had meant to instill compassion in their children for the ill child and had only succeeded in arousing frustration and the feeling that illness had its own rewards. It became clear that, if the family was to survive as a cohesive unit of people who cared for each other, everyone, including the "baby," had to respect other people's rights. The older children had to understand that they must not hurt the one who was younger and somewhat fragile, but they also had to be permitted to stop him when he got out of hand. Only in this way could he begin to see himself as a member of the family and adjust to basic rules. Though this was a hard lesson for him to learn, it was also reassuring to him to find that he was not so different from those around him. He could use his energies constructively, rather then to employ them only to annoy. The family atmosphere improved quickly. Now the older children could begin to develop the compassion for the little brother that their parents had hoped for.

THE ENFORCEMENT OF RULES

It helps to be consistent about ground rules that effect everybody, though consistency should not be confused with rigidity. Once rules have been set and explained, it is important to make sure they are adhered to, rather than to keep warning children of consequences that may never occur. In pronouncing consequences of misbehavior, it is a good idea to be careful that the consequence fits the infringement.

If a child has been forewarned and understood the situation, it is better to let him take the consequences of his action than to repeat warnings that quickly lose their effectiveness. An interesting example was demonstrated recently. A school bus driver, herself the mother of several children of various ages, found the behavior of the youngsters on the bus not only aggravating, but downright dangerous. She explained bus and safety rules to them and warned them that she would find ways to enforce the rules. This made little impression on the young, high-spirited students who were quite used to threats and to getting away with well-concerted actions. Shortly after the warning had been issued, there was a great deal of commotion on the bus. The driver made little attempt to struggle with it. On arrival at the school, she sent one child for the principal, keeping the bus closed and the rest of the children in. A hush fell over the bus. When the principal arrived, the driver explained the difficulties and the children's apparent inability to obey necessary safety rules and to observe common courtesy. She added that she would not drive these youngsters if certain basic controls were not established. The principal, though he had not been prepared for the incident, supported the driver very firmly, adding that those youngsters who found it impossible to adjust to simple rules of safety for all would have to make their own arrangements regarding getting to school. The children filed out of the bus quietly. There was no repetition of their behavior and a rather cordial, warm relationship developed between the driver and the children.

The effectiveness of this action depended on clarity, on the element of surprise, and on the collaboration of the adults involved. It made a strong impression on the children, who realized that the adults not only were in charge but were quite willing and capable of taking responsibility for the children's safety. Had the children been forewarned about what would happen, they would invariably have found ways of undercutting the effectiveness of the measure. The severity of their infractions would not have been brought home with such force.

The temptation to warn children in too much detail about what will happen "if" defeats its purpose. They may plan ahead to circumvent the course of events and may be able to build relatively small incidents into a major occurrence.

Children can do this at surprisingly young ages. I know of a six-year-old, a bright and very badly behaved little boy, who used this technique with amazing skill. His recurring question was, "What will you do if I do this?" Surprisingly, the adults always fell for this ploy and would find themselves enmeshed in this child's testing step by step whether and how threats would be carried out. The payoff came one day when he had inquired what would happen if one pulled a fire alarm. Instead of simply telling him that he was not permitted to do such a thing, his parents carefully explained to him in great detail just what would happen. They painted an exciting picture of the problem and the confusion this would create—how the fire engines would come, the traffic jams develop—the whole enticing sequence. The temptation to stand a whole area on its head with a naughty deed was too much for this child, and he did pull the alarm at the height of the rush hour in the very congested area where he lived. Everything happened as it had been explained to him. In the end, the kindly neighborhood policeman took the "cute innocent" little boy on his lap to tell him that he had been naughty and must never do something like this again. The therapist who was finally called in cut matters short very quickly by responding to the child's provocation in a simple, clear cut manner. When he wanted to know what she would do if, she told him that she would handle the situation if he misbehaved and that he might not like her way of handling it. Even the six-year-old could realize that this adult would not play the game by his rules but would be able to control him. To this he could adjust, which was a relief to him and to those around him.

THE CHANGING STRUCTURE

Discipline and structure have to change with the age and maturity of the child. If his early, pressing needs are met pleasantly and promptly, the child can gradually learn to wait for gratifications. This is where good discipline has its beginning. The hungry infant will act as if his very life is in danger if he is not fed as soon as he announces he's hungry. In a way it is. But he can learn gradually that he will survive even if the bottle is delayed for a few minutes. Eventually he learns to temper his requests, to become aware of his environment, to respond to variations in handling. Learning to wait for gratifications, to postpone them, to accept substitutes,

is perhaps the first experience with structure and discipline. Such waiting should not be imposed only for the convenience of adults, but should develop within the give and take of reasonable relationships. Such give and take soon begins to make sense even to a young child and can be accepted by him.

The child who has never been expected to absorb the simple, gradually increasing stresses of normal daily life, like waiting for a meal, managing the disappointment of a rained-out trip or not getting his turn at a game, cannot be expected to manage the pressures of a school situation. No "readiness program," no TV tutor can foster the natural ego growth that occurs through gradual enforcement of the demands of daily living within a family and among people who care and who tailor demands to the increasing ability of the maturing child.

Parents do not always find it easy to judge a child's ability to accept structure, particularly where there are several children and where there is a youngest who occupies the baby-space for ever after. It is difficult at times not to evaluate a child's age and maturity in relation to those of his siblings. Parents who assure themselves that they handle all their children the same way do not realize how unfair such a procedure would be. One cannot handle a two-year-old the same as a twelve-year-old. All of them would be in trouble. However, they also find it difficult to expect the youngest to live up to his abilities if there are older ones, and Mother knows that there won't be another one to baby and spoil after this one has grown up. The five-year-old who has three younger siblings is more readily expected to act mature and take responsibilities than the youngest when he reaches the same age. ("He's only a baby. He's only five.") Parents can become quite thoughtful on this subject when encouraged to think back to what they expected of their oldest at age five and what the oldest could deliver, when there were younger ones around who needed attention.

I remember a group discussion about table behavior of children. Restlessness at the table can be extremely trying when it comes, as it usually does, at the end of a busy, tiring day. One very well-organized mother described with surprising casualness the behavior of her quite capable two-year-old. The child apparently was constantly up and down during mealtime. To make matters worse, she was seated in a way where her comings and goings disturbed everybody. During group discussion, this mother said with real conviction that one cannot expect a two-year-old to sit through a meal. At the question, "Why not?" the whole group acted with surprise. In discussing the issues involved it became very clear that the little ones in some families indeed sat through the meal, depending on adult expectations and ability to enforce acceptable mealtime behavior. Other families felt that the struggle was too unpleasant to be worth the bother. The children were fed early or in front of the TV. They thus missed a real opportunity for learning to enjoy the one occasion during the day where the whole family could be together, when there could develop family feeling, conversation, sharing of important experiences, planning some family venture, and often an opportunity to get to know each other.

Looking at the two-year-old in question, it became obvious that part of the fun for her was disturbing everybody. The youngest of four, she had little opportunity to find herself in control of things. Her restlessness not only interfered with the mealtime of the other family members, but with her own eating. She was not interested in food if so much fun could be had by crawling under the table to get out, by having people move to let her get by, by having milk spilled as people tried to get out of the way.

The suggestion was made to talk with her prior to the next mealtime. (It is important to remember that changes in approach to a problem should always be prepared during the "cold" stage of the struggle. To scold and try to establish a change of procedure while the youngster is creating a fuss and the parent is cross will primarily create resistance and increased attempts at perpetuating the situation.) The talk with our two-year-old was to be very simple. She would be told that she was now getting to be a big girl. She had to behave like one if she wanted to eat with the family. This meant sitting down quietly like everyone else and eating. Once she left the table, this would be the end of her meal, whether she had finished or had dessert or not. The family wanted her at the table, but they did not want to be disturbed. All this was said in a friendly way and with concern for her and was quite on her level of understanding. The seating arrangement was changed so that she could leave the table without upsetting anybody. She had been seated against the wall to keep her in. Now, if she wanted to leave, nobody needed to notice, which cut down on the fun. The mother was surprised how quickly the arrangement worked. The child tried only once to leave and come back. Everybody had been cued not to pay attention to her leaving. When she tried to return she was reminded of the arrangement. When she cried that she had not had dessert, the parents were very sympathetic and comforting but stuck to their guns. There was no big re-explanation of the agreement. The child had clearly understood what it was. She wanted to be with the family and be an accepted member. She had just gotten the wrong idea about how to get attention from them. Once she began to remain at the table, she started to pay more attention to her food and to participate in table talk. The parents were careful to make sure that she was addressed and listened to and got the needed attention in a more constructive way. When she had finished eating, she was allowed to leave, while the parents still lingered over coffee. There was nothing rigid in the request that she stay put through a mealtime, though she soon showed she was ready to attend to the business at hand.

This is by no means a prescription for handling mealtime behavior problems. The point made is that, if a child's behavior is understood by the adults, it can be put in perspective and modified. It is a good idea to explore a child's ability to make adaptations. They are made by children, as by adults, in relation to the prospective rewards. A child who wants to be accepted in the family circle will try to meet expectations. If he cannot, it is worthwhile to evaluate whether expectations are too high, or to understand, as in our case here, whether the disruption is more pleasure than cooperation is. When the pleasure of disruption was minimized by the structure developed, the child was given the opportunity to find out that cooperation could be more rewarding.

Should a somewhat older child decide to show the parents that he did not care to be included in the family circle and ask to be excluded, this too could be arranged without rancor, but also without making the arrangement too comfortable. Normally, no child will really treasure exclusion from the family, even if it is self-imposed. Return to the family group should be made easy for such a child and he should always know that he is missed. If he persists in staying away, the real reason for his voluntary exile should be determined quickly.

Modifications will need to be considered without playing into a child's unhealthy control of the family. The most important first step would have to be to understand why the child is acting in a basically self-punishing way, what has gone wrong in relationships, at least in the child's mind, and what modifications can be made that would satisfy both the child and the rest of the family. Mutual consideration and planning are the best ways to change the situation.

PREPARATION FOR CHANGES

If changes in handling become indicated for whatever reason, the child should always be a party to the decisions, however young he is. As was shown in the previous example, even the two-year-old could understand what was being planned and had time to adjust her own approach. Making the child a party to arrangements, increases the chances for success. As stated before, trying to establish changes while the parties are in the midst of an argument seldom works. Everybody is angry at that stage, resistant to change and unwilling to consider the possibility that the other party may have a point. This is not a good precondition for cool consideration and willingness to modify one's own approach. If everybody has reached the limit of his endurance, parents may have to establish the new rules and regulations immediately. However, if difficulties have persisted for a while, one can easily wait another day to make the change.

Morning routines provide good illustrations of situations where changes need to be established. Mornings are likely to be times of stress, rush, and turmoil. The fact that there are "morning people" and "night people," those who are ready to go as soon as they open their eyes and those who are not ready for action until late in the day, does not really change this fact. The presence of both in one family will just increase the confusion. It is very tempting for children to take advantage of the morning preoccupations to try to establish control over the situation. Children know early that morning time is precious, and that there are top priorities such as father's departure for work or school or bus schedules to be met. They may pick this time for creating problems, annoying sleepy adults or siblings. The rambunctious child himself may not be at his best in the early morning and feel entitled to special privilege, as does everybody else.

On exploring such situations in detail, one will often find that morning schedules are not schedules at all, but have just grown, like Topsy. They are frequently set up in a way that invites trouble. Children, up early, have turned on the TV and cannot be lured away. The late riser cannot be lured out of bed. Children traipse down for breakfast without having washed or dressed, and then dawdle over eating, over dressing and over other morning routines, leaving Mother to take responsibility for the weather, everyone's schedules, finding lost shoes, and arguing over what pants, dress, or socks each child should wear. A few ground rules set early, and organization and preperation in the evening when things are calmer, may go a long way to relax the morning. Preparation in the evening for the next day can be a pleasurable, relaxed activity between parents and children. It is good to explain to a child early in the game what his responsibility toward getting ready will be. Even the pre-schooler can lay out his own nursery school clothing the day before. He will enjoy selecting what he will wear. Short of wanting to wear heavy dungarees during a hot spell, or a flimsy dress in winter, the choice could be the child's, even if he chooses purple socks with green shorts. The very pleasure of selecting his own clothing and putting it into a predesignated place will prevent a fight over what to wear in the morning. A sweater or raincoat can always be added, if needed. It is important, however, that parents, once they have told a child that he can select his own things, not become manipulative because they do not like the youngster's choice.

Another helpful plan is to ban TV in the morning, and serve no breakfast to pajama'd children. Once the child is washed and dressed, he is more likely to be awake and has less opportunity to dawdle and delay. Evening preparation for the morning after helps with organization that can be achieved only with difficulty in the early morning when some people are sleepy and all are rushed. I have found that at times even good homemakers realize, during discussion of morning routine, that they leave clothing in the dryer to be picked out in the morning or shoes out in the rain, or find all the underpants in the laundry hamper at 7:00 AM. Preparation in the evening leaves time for remedies right then and teaches the children some simple, helpful habits early.

INDEPENDENCE AND MANIPULATION

As was discussed earlier, structure and habit training go a long way in helping a child toward healthy, age-appropriate independence. Independence and the development of judgment have to develop slowly and naturally. However, apparently prompted by adult anxiety, there is a tendency now to push children's independence from adults at ever-earlier ages. There is a surprising idea that judgment is developed by leaving children to make their own choices long before they have any idea what the choices are and what the consequences of one choice over the other would be. Pushing too early independence and leaving children floundering regarding their choices or taking guidance from the TV creates the impression that the adults are about to abdicate their responsibility in relation to the child. The possibilities of making the wrong choice are almost endless, and the learning potential from mistakes is rather limited. The child who is left too much to make his own choices and has been stung too often by the consequences is inclined to become self-limiting and rigid regarding choices. He is not interested in trying new things and will be inclined to use his freedom of choice to insist that he may do only what he already knows.

The two-year-old cannot possibly know what foods he likes and what tastes he will develop until he has had much opportunity not only to taste but to eat repeatedly a great variety. If the choice is left entirely to him, he will stick with what he knows, play havoc with nutrition, and miss a great deal of enjoyment. He will forego not only treats for his tastebuds, but the enjoyment of being a welcome guest at someone else's dinner table, if he eats only hamburgers with catsup.

The four- or six-year-old does not have nearly enough experience to select clothing to be bought, and even the teenager who has been going to school for quite a while is not quite ready to choose his school curriculum.

To involve children in choices that affect them, to listen to their preferences, will gradually help them develop the ability to make decisions. A voice in council and some veto rights may do at the beginning. The five-year-old who still lives on milk, ice cream, and cookies and gets his nutritional requirements from the drugstore will grow up into a rather queer specimen, even if doctors tell us that vitamin needs can be covered by a pill. The child will miss the fun of biting into a crunchy apple, the delight of the various tastes of imaginatively prepared vegetables, the enjoyment of the Thanksgiving feast, and he will not be a welcome guest chewing quietly at his vitamins after the hostess has spent thought and time preparing a festive meal.

Parents who like to boast about the maturity of their offspring, who make their own decisions at an amazingly young age, are quite aware that the youngster's immature decisions can be highly inconvenient or downright counterindicated. If they have prematurely built up the child's conviction that the decision-making and choice are entirely his, the adult is likely to resort to manipulation rather than to clarification of roles and responsibilities with a confused child. It is exactly this manipulation that leads to the tension between parent and child that makes the parent throw up his hands and exclaim that he does not understand what the child wants since he *is* free to make his own selections and choices. Children may openly question a clear-cut decision they do not like. If relationships are good, there can be discussion, modification of a situation, or a final decision against the child's wishes if necessary. Manipulation, which is an underground maneuver, is hard to fight but is often met by the child with similar countermeasures. The child feels helpless and frustrated in the face of adult manipulation. He is only dimly aware of what is occurring. He realizes a dishonesty, but he doesn't quite know what the game is. Seemingly unreasonable violent temper outbursts on the part of the child are often the consequence of adult manipulation. Manipulated children frequently insist rigidly on their own rights, even if they realize the adult's decision is the better choice. They are inclined to be dissatisfied and blame the environment if their own choices backfire.

A situation that sticks vividly in my mind occurred with friends of mine. The mother in the situation had highly intellectualized concepts of child rearing. "Children," she said, "have to be permitted their own choices. My child [age 8] is allowed to pick her own clothing. I go with her and I will say, 'Look at this lovely blue coat. You look so well in blue,' and the child will take the blue coat, and everyone is happy." No one was really happy. This little girl had disturbing daily problems about what to wear. The "independently" selected coat or dress would gather dust in the closet, and Mother and child were at constant war, which puzzled the mother, who felt that she did everything to make her daughter happy.

I have seen much happier shopping trips when mother permitted the youngster to decide among the three or four items she had selected, and which fitted her pocketbook and her judgment of quality and suitability of style. This mother could then occasionally give in to a passionately desired purchase that did not meet her approval. She could permit the child an occasional error in judgment. If the child recognized his error, there was no further discussion. The lesson had been learned. She was actually training the youngster to recognize quality and suitability with the child's honest and conscious cooperation.

The same kind of approach is helpful in all areas of developing judgment. This, in the early years, will center around food, permissibility of activities, straying from home, etc. Later there comes the choice of friends, activities with contemporaries, selection of school subjects, and so on. The list could be long. The gradual development of judgment, the ability to know what the options are and to make choices, is undramatic, like all gradual training and development. But this kind of development will provide a better base for solid development of personality. The assumption that we learn by making mistakes is only partially correct. Only correctable mistakes add up to experience. Serious and continuos errors can be quite damaging to the developing child. They can instill in him a discouraging picture of himself as unable to do anything right. We allow children on the one hand to get into serious difficulties by pushing them prematurely into making choices; on the other hand, we overprotect them against making mistakes that are not devastating but would lend themselves quite well to learning and developing judgment about their own abilities and limits. For instance, to permit a six-year-old to decide on his own diet can have serious consequences. Not to interfere in his engaging in an angry tussle with someone twice his size, however, will add up to experience.

To guide a child in his judgments, commiserate with him if he has erred, help him to anticipate the consequences of his behavior, and assist him in his ability to acknowledge and correct errors are important adult responsibilities. Success in carrying them out is based on mutual respect and trust between adult and child.

CONCLUSIONS

And so again: "What is a parent to do?"

If we want the next generation—and the next and the next—to develop into responsive and responsible human beings, and not into mechanized, programed automatons, we have to assure children human guidance, however inadequate it may be. If it springs from human love and interest it will meet the needs. We cannot abdicate to machines and leave it to them to train our children. We cannot expose children to computerized "right or "wrong" type reactions to the complex world around them. We cannot allow children to become statistical data filed away into neat cubbyholes like so many animal experiments.

TV and radio do not have an independent life of their own. They can be turned off. This is and has to be an adult decision. In the ensuing quiet one might reestablish the fraying pattern of family life. Conversation and dialogue may reemerge as a bridge toward knowledge of each other and toward relationships not influenced by mechanical solutions to the neat little problems of a mechanical society.

Cognitive information is important to children. It will fascinate a generation growing up surrounded by machinery that seems to simplify the overwhelming complexities of their live environment. Cognitive knowledge lends itself to easy, neat tabulation for quick results. Some of what children need to know can apparently be taught by machines. But cognitive knowledge can be acquired at almost any stage of life. It is best acquired when the individual child is ready and has application for what he is learning. This is true even if the machine that dispenses the "knowledge" can be manipulated by a toddler. The machine can dispense knowledge; it cannot time it to meet readiness and needs, which are prerequisites for the ability to integrate knowledge. That the acquisition of facts is not limited to the first few years of life is demonstrated by the grandmothers who return to college when they are ready for a career. They seem quite able to absorb information they missed several decades earlier.

In contrast, the development of human qualities cannot be delayed nor can it be accomplished by machinery. It has to be experienced and lived through in orderly stages that have their own sequence, even if they seem uneven and meandering. The space and time needed for this slow process must not be preempted by the push and shove for early cognition.

"What's a parent to do?" And what is an educator to do? And what is everyone to do who is not only interested in children, but really likes them and is concerned about the world into which they have to grow?

We have to take time for children. We have to live with and through them, not beside them. We have to enjoy them, not by being amused by their shortcomings, but by recognizing these shortcomings as important steps in their development. These steps can be exciting and constructive if properly channeled.

Real concern for children cannot be taught in college courses. Courses in Human Relations and Parent Effectiveness and Sensitivity have their place. They help with the intellectual understanding of these phenomena. Child development and aspects of child behavior can be taught in classes. The matrix for proper application of what has been learned is parental love. It is the main ingredient in understanding children and meeting their needs. It is the seed from which springs the child's love for his parents that makes him accessible to parental and eventually all external influences.

Parents need feedback from their investment in their children. The child will repay the parents by loving them and by developing well. But this is sometimes a slow, almost imperceptible process, and parents may need support from outside sources. They may need to have someone tell them that they are doing well, or they may need assistance in finding their way in the maze of possible right and wrong turns in trying to help their children grow. Today's young parents usually lack the natural support of their own primary families, their parents and their siblings, as well as aunts, uncles, cousins. They may be in need of professionals who can supply this support. The average parent, caught in his own insecurity, usually does not need complicated therapy, but practical guidance in selecting that approach that will best aid him and his family. He needs the encouragement that what he is doing is helpful.

Parent groups, developed with this goal in mind, can provide sounding boards, opportunity to exchange thoughts and mutual support among the members. Such groups, contrary to some popular belief, do need expert leadership if they are not to deteriorate into exchanges of ignorance. But the leader needs to remain carefully aware of the purpose of the group, which should not be treatment of pathology nor interpretation of deep-seated problems. Half-digested interpretations as to underlying reasons for one's actions are too easily used as an excuse to continue a faulty approach rather than as a lever toward change. The parent who has serious emotional problems needs a different kind of therapy. Parents who suffer from the normal anxieties and bafflement of our current hectic daily life can gain perspective on their own approaches in a parent group, learn what works in other similar families and what can be modified for home consumption. They can learn about new approaches to family and child management and gain support from knowing that they are not alone in being bemused and nonplussed by some of their offspring's antics.

Groups in which parents and children have an opportunity for joint participation have been tried with success. With competent leadership and sufficient time parents and children have opportunity to play and talk with each other. The parents learn techniques of participating in their youngsters' activities, enjoy successes in a given activity, and experience frustrations that remind them how hard it can be for the child not to master a task. They learn to handle their children's squabbles and other daily emergencies with some equanimity. Time and emotions are freed to give love instead of finding it buried under small irritations.

Local guidance centers could be developed to become part of neighborhoods, offering opportunity for informal chats and prevention of difficulties. If these centers are part of the daily scene, they will certainly be used. They should be part of any kind of neighborhood, the well-established one as well as the troubled one. Such centers could serve a real purpose for all economic and ethnic groups. They would need to be staffed by various helping professions as well as neighborhood workers who could augment each others' approaches and skills. There should be those professionals who can relate to parental needs, and those who are concerned with children's needs, as well as representatives from the health services. Together they could supply support and services with a focus on the fairly stable, well-functioning family. They could also serve as a resource and referral center for those families that are more troubled and need more specialized services.

Such an endeavor would not be highly dramatic, but stabilizing and enabling in its function. Funding for such a center might be hard to obtain, but in the long run a preventative program is much less expensive than a program designed to treat after damage has occurred. Small wounds heal more easily and leave smaller scars.

Children have ecological value way beyond any other endangered species. We have to remain intricately involved with them, struggle with them when necessary, meet their protests and resistance, and help them and ourselves to put things into perspective. We have to modify our own approaches to meet a new world and help them to modify their expectations to handle a current reality. It is adult responsibility to help children find their own way in the bewildering maze that constitutes our lives.

SUGGESTED READING

Ames, Louise Bates, "Don't Push your Pre-Schooler," *Family Circle,* December 1971.

Axline, Virginia M., *Dibs in Search of Self,* Ballantine Books, New York, 1967.

Beck, Helen L., *Going to Camp,* Stephen Daye Press, New York, 1949.

Coles, Robert, and Piers, Maria, *Wages of Neglect,* Quadrangle Books, New York, 1969.

Erikson, Erik, *Childhood and Society,* W. W. Norton & Co., New York, 1963.

Francke, Linda, "The Games People Play on Sesame Street," *New York Magazine,* April 5, 1971.

Freud, Anna, *The Ego and the Mechanism of Defense,* International Universities Press, New York, 1946.

Hall, Elizabeth, "A Conversation with Piaget," *Psychology Today,* May 1971.

Hawkins, David, "On Understanding the Understanding of Children," *American Journal of Diseases of Children,* November 1967.

Hesse, Hermann, *Beneath the Wheel,* Noonday Press, New York, 1969.

Holt, John, "Big Bird Meet Dick and Jane," *Atlantic Monthly,* May 1971.

Le Shane, Eda, *The Conspiracy Against Childhood,* Atheneum Publishers, New York, 1968.

Morgenstern, Joseph, "Children's Hour," *Newsweek,* August 16, 1971.

Krug, Othilda, and Beck, Helen L., *A Guide to Better Discipline,* Science Research Associates, Chicago, 1954.

Paul, Norman L., "Invisible Factors in a Child's Reaction to TV," *Childhood Education,* March 1971.

Suggested Reading

Ribble, Margaret, *The Rights of Infants,* Columbia University Press, New York, 1965.

Robbins, Melvyn, "Test of the Doman-Delacato Rationale with Retarded Readers," *Journal of the American Medical Association,* October 1967.

Skinner, B. F., *Beyond Freedom and Dignity,* Alfred A. Knopf, New York, 1971.

Publication of the American Academy of Pediatrics, "Obedience: Means Safety for Your Child," 1960.

ABOUT THE AUTHOR

HELEN L. BECK was born in Vienna. She became a successful teacher in nursery and elementary schools there and a
member of the Psychoanalytic Institute of Vienna. In 1938,
she went to England and there developed a wartime day
nursery. In 1940 Miss Beck came to the United States,
taught nursery school, and did group work until she received her MS in Social Work from Bryn Mawr. She then
worked as a social worker, at family agencies, and in vari
ous psychiatric settings. For ten years she was Chief Psy
chiatric Social Worker for neurologically handicapped
children at St. Christopher's Hospital for Children in
Philadelphia and an Associate Professor in their Department of Pediatrics.

Miss Beck now lives in Connecticut where she is a
school social worker for the Westport Board of Education.